MASSACHUSETTS WILDLIFE VIEWING GUIDE

William J. Davis, Massachusetts Division of Fisheries & Wildlife

FALCON

Helena, Montana

ACKNOWLEDGMENTS

The list of people who contributed ideas and site nominations, provided peer review, and were the driving force behind this guide would include more than 200 names. While space limitations will not permit individual recognition here, their time, effort, and devotion to the guide is reflected in the finished product. Special thanks to all who participated.

The Massachusetts Watchable Wildlife Steering Committee provided direction, insight, and consistency in producing the *Massachusetts Wildlife Viewing Guide*. Sincere thanks go to Jack Buckley of the Division of Fisheries & Wildlife (DFW), Tom Skinner of the Executive Office of Environmental Affairs (EOEA), Jack Lash and Karl Honkonen from the Department of Environmental Management (DEM), Kevin Hollenbeck of the Metropolitan District Commission (MDC), Tom Tyning of the Massachusetts Audubon Society (MAS), Lisa Vernegaard of The Trustees of Reservations (TTOR), Janet Kennedy of the U.S. Fish and Wildlife Service (USFWS), Patrice Todisco of the Massachusetts Highway Department (MHD), Jane Howes of the Massachusetts Office of Travel and Tourism (MOTT), and Rick Magee of the U. S. Army Corps of Engineers (USACE) for their quality input.

Other invaluable assistance was provided by the field and administrative staffs of the agencies and organizations listed above. I am particularly grateful to the personnel of the DFW's Natural Heritage and Endangered Species Program, 5 Wildlife District Offices, and the Information and Education Section for their support. Additionally, Brad Blodget, Tom French, Bob Madore, and Collette Cadieux of the DFW, Rich Lombardi of EOEA, Susan Ziegler of DEM, Clif Read and Paul Lyons of the MDC, John Bradley of MAS, Kate Wollensak of TTOR, Carolyn Boardman of the USFWS, Julie Vitek of MHD, Ken Garber of Northeast Utilities (NU), Bill Burke and Mike Reynolds of the National Park Service (NPS), Karen Combs-Beattie of the Nantucket Conservation Foundation (NCF), John O'Keefe of the Harvard Forest, and Mark Mello of the Lloyd Center for Environmental Studies made significant contributions. DFW Senior Wildlife Photographer Bill Byrne and Illustrator Terri Talas brought the guide to life with their combined artistic talents.

My wife, Dianne, and our children, Becky and Ben, share my fascination with nature. Watching wildlife through their eyes added new perspective to wonderful sights.

Finally, Wildlife Viewing Guide Program Manager Kate Davies and Falcon Press editors Eric Keszler and John Grassy provided guidance, support, and infinite patience throughout the project.

Author and State Project Manager:
William J. Davis, MA Division of Fisheries & Wildlife

Viewing Guide Program Manager:
Kate Davies, Defenders of Wildlife

Illustrator:
Terri Talas

All photos by Bill Byrne, MA Division of Fisheries & Wildlife
Front cover: Breaching humpback whale
Back cover: White-tailed deer & blooming rhododendrons

CONTENTS

REGION 4: NORTHEAST

REGION 5: SOUTHEAST

PROJECT SPONSORS

The *Massachusetts Wildlife Viewing Guide* sponsors listed below are dedicated to promoting wildlife and wildlife habitat in Massachusetts. If you would like to join them by becoming a volunteer or member, making a donation, or supporting a specific property, contact the appropriate agency or organization at the address or telephone number provided. Most sponsors have "Friends" groups to encourage volunteerism and trust funds to accept financial support.

 The MASSACHUSETTS DIVISION OF FISHERIES & WILDLIFE (DFW) is responsible for the conservation of fish, wildlife, wild plant, and natural community resources in the commonwealth. The DFW seeks to balance the diversity of wildlife populations and their habitats with the best interests of the public and to provide wildlife-related recreation and education. More than 80,000 acres are actively managed to enhance wildlife habitat and provide public access to open space. The DFW produces a quarterly magazine, *Massachusetts Wildlife*. For more information, contact the Division of Fisheries & Wildlife, Field Headquarters, Westboro, MA 01581-9990; (508) 792-7270.

 DEFENDERS OF WILDLIFE is a national nonprofit organization of more than 100,000 members and supporters dedicated to preserving the natural abundance and diversity of wildlife and its habitat. A one-year membership is $20 and includes a subscription to *Defenders,* an award-winning conservation magazine. To join or for further information, write or call Defenders of Wildlife, 1101 14th Street, NW, Suite 1400, Washington, DC 20005, (202) 682-9400.

 The MASSACHUSETTS DEPARTMENT OF ENVIRONMENTAL MANAGEMENT (DEM) is the largest public landowner in Massachusetts, with stewardship responsibilities for more than 100 state forests, parks, beaches, and reservations totaling more than 280,000 acres. DEM has the dual mission of oversight for the natural, cultural, and historic resources of the Commonwealth while providing quality recreational opportunities which are environmentally sound, affordable, and accessible to the public. For additional information, contact the Department of Environmental Management, 100 Cambridge Street, Boston, MA 02202; (617) 727-3180.

 The METROPOLITAN DISTRICT COMMISSION (MDC) is a multi-service state agency responsible for the management and stewardship of the natural, cultural, and recreational resources of the greater Boston area. The MDC manages a 19,405-acre urban park system and 120,000 acres of reservoir and watershed lands that provide clean drinking water to 2.5 million Massachusetts residents. For further information, contact the Metropolitan District Commission, Public Information Office, 20 Somerset Street, Boston, MA 02108; (617) 727-5114.

 The MASSACHUSETTS EXECUTIVE OFFICE OF ENVIRONMENTAL AFFAIRS (EOEA) oversees state policies and programs that protect the natural resources of the Commonwealth. EOEA prioritizes the areas of resource protection, streamlining the environmental regulatory process and promoting environmentally sound or "green" business. The DFW, DEM, MDC, and Departments of Environmental Protection and Food and Agriculture function within EOEA. For more information, contact the Executive Office of Environmental Affairs, 100 Cambridge Street, Boston, MA 02202; (617) 727-3160.

 The MASSACHUSETTS HIGHWAY DEPARTMENT (MHD) and its 2,300 employees are responsible for the design, maintenance, and construction of the state's 4,500 bridges and over 12,000 lane miles of highway. MHD strives to upgrade, modernize, and rebuild the highways with a higher degree of efficiency, environmental protection, and economic gain for the commonwealth. In recent years, MHD has overseen more than 500 construction projects, including the Central Artery/Third Harbor Tunnel, the largest public works project in North America.

 The MASSACHUSETTS OFFICE OF TRAVEL AND TOURISM (MOTT) is responsible for promoting Massachusetts as a travel destination from both domestic and international markets. The agency manages a year-round advertising program and provides marketing support and technical assistance to Massachusetts' travel businesses and tourism organizations. For more information, contact the Massachusetts Office of Travel and Tourism, 100 Cambridge Street, Boston, MA 02202; (617) 727-3201; www. mass–vacation.com.

 The U.S. FISH AND WILDLIFE SERVICE (USFWS) is the principal federal agency responsible for conserving, protecting, and enhancing the nation's fish and wildlife and their habitats for the benefit, use, and enjoyment of the American people. For further information, contact the U.S. Fish and Wildlife Service, 300 Westgate Center Drive, Hadley, MA 01035-9589; (413) 253-8200.

 The U.S. ARMY CORPS OF ENGINEERS (USACE) is the steward of over 24,500 acres of lands and waters in Massachusetts at twelve flood control reservoirs, the Charles River Natural Valley Storage Area, and the Cape Cod Canal. The USACE joins with its visitors to promote the conservation and enjoyment of fish and wildlife on Corps properties. For more information, contact the U.S. Army Corps of Engineers, Lower Connecticut River Basin Office, 6 Athol-Richmond Road, Royalston, MA 01331.

 The NATIONAL PARK SERVICE (NPS) is charged with administering the units of the National Park System in a manner that protects and conserves their natural and cultural resources for the enjoyment of present and future generations. In Massachusetts, the NPS administers over 10 units. For more information, contact the National Park Service, 15 State Street, Boston, MA 02109; (617) 223-5199.

The MASSACHUSETTS AUDUBON SOCIETY (MAS), formed in 1896, is one of the oldest and largest conservation organizations in New England. The society operates 35 sanctuaries, protects more than 25,000 acres of conservation land/wildlife habitat, provides nature programs for 200,000 students annually, and advocates for sound environmental policies. For more information, contact Massachusetts Audubon Society, South Great Road, Lincoln, MA 01773; (617) 259-9500.

 THE TRUSTEES OF RESERVATIONS (TTOR), founded in 1891, is the world's oldest regional land trust. It is a member-supported, non-profit land conservation organization dedicated to preserving properties of exceptional scenic, historic, and ecological value. TTOR owns and manages 77 properties, including historic houses, forest, salt marsh, and beaches, totaling more than 20,000 acres. An additional 10,000 acres are protected through the use of conservation restrictions. For additional information, contact The Trustees of Reservations, Public Information, 290 Argilla

Road, P.O. Box 563, Ipswich, MA 01938; (508) 356-4351.

 NORTHEAST UTILITIES (NU) is New England's largest electric utility, serving customers from the Connecticut shore to the Canadian border through western Massachusetts and the state of New Hampshire. NU has long taken a strong stewardship role by incorporating a broad range of environmental initiatives within its operations and service area. To learn more about its environmental performance, please write to Corporate and Environmental Affairs, Northeast Utilities Service Company, P.O. Box 270, Hartford, CT 06141.

 TENNECO ENERGY, headquartered in Houston, is one of the nation's largest natural gas pipeline companies. It transports or markets more than 3.2 trillion cubic feet of gas annually, approximately 15 percent of total U.S. consumption, through its 18,300-mile domestic pipeline system. Internationally, Tenneco Energy is active in energy infrastructure projects in Australia, Latin America, Central Europe, and East Asia. The company's other major business interests include Tenneco Packaging, Tenneco Automotive, and Newport News Shipbuilding. For additional information, contact Tenneco, Suite 300, 25 Burlington Mall Road, Burlington, MA 01803.

DEPARTMENT OF DEFENSE (DOD) is a steward of about 25 million acres of land in the United States, many of which possess irreplaceable natural and cultural resources. The DOD is pleased to support the Watchable Wildlife Program through its Legacy Resource Management Program, a special initiative to enhance the conservation and restoration of natural and cultural resources on military land. For more information contact the Office of the Deputy Under Secretary of Defense (Environmental Security), 400 Navy Drive, Suite 206, Arlington, VA 22202-2884.

OTHER IMPORTANT SPONSORS INCLUDE:

New England Electric System, Harvard University, Lloyd Center for Environmental Studies, Nantucket Conservation Foundation, National Oceanic and Atmospheric Administration, and Massachusetts Division of Environmental Law Enforcement

Copyright ©1996 by Falcon Press® Publishing Co., Inc., Helena and Billings, Montana.

Published in cooperation with Defenders of Wildlife.

All rights reserved, including the right to reproduce this book or any part thereof in any form, except brief quotations for reviews, without written permission of the publisher.

Design, typesetting, and other prepress work by Falcon Press®, Helena, Montana. Printed in Korea.

Defenders of Wildlife and its design are registered marks of Defenders of Wildlife, Washington, D.C.

Watchable Wildlife® is a registered trademark of Falcon Press® Publishing Co., Inc.

Library of Congress Cataloging-in-Publication Data
Davis, William J., 1958-
    Massachusetts wildlife viewing guide / William J. Davis
      p. cm.
    Includes index.
    ISBN 1-56044-426-6 (pbk.)
    1. Wildlife viewing sites—Massachusetts—Guidebooks. 2. Wildlife watching—Massachusetts—Guidebooks. 3. Massachusetts—Guidebooks.
I. Title.
QL183.D38 1997
599.09744—dc20

96-36433
CIP

The Commonwealth of Massachusetts
Executive Department
State House - Boston 02133

Dear Friends:

From the summit of Mount Greylock to the offshore depths of Stellwagen Bank, everything from warblers to whales inhabits Massachusetts' wild lands and waters. Diverse fauna and flora thrive in the rich hills and woodlands of the Berkshires and along the picturesque beaches and inlets of Cape Ann, Cape Cod, and the Islands. Cities and towns throughout the Commonwealth support thriving parks and waterways that are home to delicate ecosystems. Since the Commonwealth's earliest days, Massachusetts citizens and visitors have enjoyed and valued its unique natural beauty.

The *Massachusetts Wildlife Viewing Guide* will help you better understand and identify the Commonwealth's birds, fish, and animals. This handbook provides important and interesting information about our various wildlife species—numbering over 600—and the distinct habitats that sustain them.

Lieutenant Governor Cellucci and I encourage you to enjoy, respect, and protect Massachusetts' natural areas, as they are a valuable link to our past and a vital key to our future.

Sincerely,

Bin Weld

William F. Weld

INTRODUCTION

The Commonwealth of Massachusetts is renowned for its sense of history, cultural treasures, and scenic beauty. Images of the Pilgrims landing at Plymouth, Nathaniel Hawthorne's *House of the Seven Gables* in Salem, or a quaint town common framed with colorful autumn foliage are all readily associated with the Bay State.

Just off the beaten path, Massachusetts is also home to many equally impressive natural wonders. Central among these are the many species of wildlife inhabiting our woods, waters, and open spaces. Many an outdoor activity has been enhanced by the sighting of a wary white-tailed deer, brilliant cardinal, or ponderous snapping turtle. Children are especially drawn to wildlife and can be awed by the fragile beauty of a butterfly, the geometric precision of a spider web, or the absolute patience of a bullfrog.

Trips and outings for the specific purpose of watching wildlife are becoming increasingly popular. In fact, figures compiled by the U.S. Fish and Wildlife Service indicate almost 30 million Americans go on wildlife viewing trips each year. To help

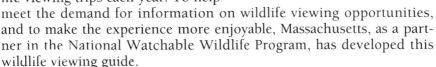

CHICKADEE

meet the demand for information on wildlife viewing opportunities, and to make the experience more enjoyable, Massachusetts, as a partner in the National Watchable Wildlife Program, has developed this wildlife viewing guide.

The guide provides helpful hints on how and when to watch wildlife, along with descriptions of 67 viewing sites, their facilities, special attractions, telephone numbers for up-to-date site information, and detailed directions. Use the material presented here to plan a wildlife viewing trip and to make the most of your time in the field, whether it be going on a coastal whale watch, looking for wintering bald eagles, or just spending an hour in a nearby park.

There's something for every wildlife enthusiast, from the beginner to the experienced naturalist, to be found outdoors in Massachusetts. Take advantage of the sites listed here and discover the scores of others that are your gateway to wildlife watching.

Authors, artists, and photographers spend lifetimes trying to capture and express their impressions of wildlife and the outdoors. There is no substitute, however, for a firsthand encounter with a wild animal in its natural environment. Enjoy and share an outdoor experience with family and friends and help conserve Massachusetts' natural areas by supporting the agencies and organizations working on behalf of wildlife and the habitats critical to their survival.

THE NATIONAL WATCHABLE WILDLIFE PROGRAM

In response to the growing interest in wildlife viewing, Massachusetts has joined the National Watchable Wildlife partnership by bringing together a coalition of state, federal, private, and business interests to promote environmental stewardship. The National Watchable Wildlife Program consists of: 1) a network of wildlife viewing sites, 2) a uniform system of road signs directing travelers to wildlife viewing sites, and 3) the wildlife viewing guide series. Massachusetts' Watchable Wildlife Program will use the viewing sites and guide as tools to foster increased environmental awareness, conservation, and education, and to bring the public closer to the natural world around them.

The partnership will continue at both the national and state level, beyond the production of the *Massachusetts Wildlife Viewing Guide*, by enhancing many viewing sites with platforms, boardwalks, trails, interpretive materials, and directional signs featuring the brown-and-white binocular logo appearing on the cover of this guide. Other sites will remain virtually untouched, giving the wildlife viewer many options for wildlife viewing trips.

CHIPMUNK

The goal of the program is to build support for wildlife and habitat by encouraging people to enjoy, firsthand, wildlife viewing experiences in natural surroundings. From those encounters a sense of excitement, understanding, and pride should emerge, leading to increased participation in conservation efforts and increased support of the groups leading those efforts. Such support can only lead to a brighter future for wildlife at the local, state, national, and global levels.

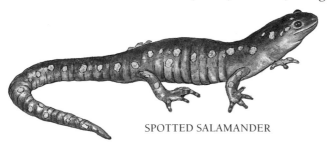

SPOTTED SALAMANDER

HOW TO USE THIS GUIDE

Your *Massachusetts Wildlife Viewing Guide* is your introduction to 67 special places across the Commonwealth. To make the most of your wildlife viewing opportunities, use the guide to plan your trips and enhance your visits. Please familiarize yourself with the contents and format of the guide so you'll be able to take advantage of the information provided.

The first part of the guide contains a list of the featured sites, a state road and site map, a key to the site facility icons, and sections with tips and ideas for safe, successful, and ethical wildlife viewing. The body of the guide is divided into 5 sections, each representing a geographical region of the state. Each regional section is prefaced by a description of the area including a more detailed road map and a list of the sites within that region. Listed sites are numbered to correspond to locations on the statewide and regional maps.

Site descriptions contain the site number and name, a general **description** of the habitat and features, and a more detailed discussion of the wildlife under the heading of **viewing information**. **Directions** are provided to lead the viewer to the site from state roadways identified on the maps. These directions should be supplemented with current state maps, a road atlas, and, in some cases, topographic maps. **Ownership** and/or the managing agency are listed with a contact telephone number for additional information. The **size** of each site is given, as is the **closest town** where food, fuel, pay phone, and other services are available. **Icons** identifying the facilities and recreational options at each site are given at the end of each site description.

PUMPKINSEED

Photographs and artwork, with accompanying captions and text, are found throughout the guide. Interesting facts, figures, and viewing hints appear with the Watchable Wildlife binocular logo along the bottom margin of some pages.

KEY TO FACILITIES AND RECREATION

The following icons represent facilities and recreational opportunities available at sites where the icon is listed. These are general guidelines and may have local or seasonal restrictions and limitations. Call ahead for site-specific facilities information.

Parking	Entry Fee or Use Fee	Restrooms	Barrier-Free	Picnic	Interpretive Programs	Fishing	Camping

Hiking	Cross-Country Skiing	Bicycling	Boat Ramp	Motorized Boats	Non-motorized Boats	Horse Trails	Hunting

11

VIEWING ETHICS AND SAFETY

Wildlife is a public resource, managed by public agencies for the benefit of the resource and people alike. As a member of the public, you share responsibility for conserving these wildlife resources. Part of this responsibility involves being an ethical and safe wildlife watcher, combining common sense and common courtesy in your approach to wildlife and your fellow viewers. Here are some simple guidelines for ethical and safe viewing:

- Keep a reasonable distance from wildlife, using your binoculars and spotting scope, rather than your feet, to "get closer" to your subject. If you get too close to an animal its behavior will change. It may stop feeding, look at you, vocalize, appear nervous, or flee. If you note a change in behavior, back off slowly until you're out of the animal's "space."

- Be a responsible steward of the land, both public and private. Follow marked trails where indicated and leave an area cleaner than you found it. Get permission before entering private land.

- Show consideration for other wildlife watchers. Speak quietly, move cautiously, and don't use tapes or calls that might interfere with the viewing experience. Leave pets at home (many wildlife areas prohibit them).

WHITE-TAILED DEER

- Leave seemingly abandoned wildlife alone. Young mammals and birds may appear to be orphaned when actually there is an adult waiting nearby until it is safe to return. Never feed wildlife.

- Become active with a conservation group, land trust, or conservation commission and participate in environmental activities. As you learn about the outdoors, share your knowledge with others, especially children.

- Keep safety in mind when you venture outdoors. Whenever possible, use the "buddy system" and go wildlife watching with a friend. Sharing the experience is twice as fun.

- Let someone know where you are going and when you plan to return. Carry a small first-aid kit, weatherproof matches, compass, and a space blanket in your pack.

- Keep an eye on the weather. New England is notorious for sudden weather changes. Seek safe shelter when storms approach.

- Familiarize yourself with when and where activities like hunting, off-road-vehicle and personal watercraft use are permitted. Having this information and planning accordingly can eliminate potential conflicts between wildlife watching and other outdoor recreation.

- Report violations of wildlife laws to site managers and the Massachusetts Environmental Police 1-800-632-8075.

PLANNING A WILDLIFE VIEWING TRIP

A little advance planning will result in a more enjoyable, comfortable, and successful wildlife viewing trip. Before leaving home, review the accounts given in this guide and call ahead to check on current viewing opportunities, access restrictions, and facilities, or to make reservations for tours and interpretive programs. Consider the area you plan to visit and make a checklist of essential items: binoculars, sunscreen, sunglasses, hat, appropriate footwear, layers of clothing, road maps, topographic maps, insect repellent, snacks, drinks, etc. If you're properly prepared you'll be able to stay in the field longer, increasing your chances of seeing wildlife.

Don't be disappointed if you don't see everything a viewing site has to offer. Rather, enjoy the animals and scenery you do see, and learn as much about the site and its wild residents as possible. It will often take several trips to a particular site to become familiar with the terrain and the habits of the wildlife.

As you travel throughout the Bay State, take advantage of the many historical, cultural, educational, and natural attractions available. Combining a wildlife viewing trip with your other interests makes for great day trips, weekends, and vacations. For some ideas and a travel guide contact the Massachusetts Office of Travel and Tourism at (617)727-3201 or via their web site: www.mass–vacation.com.

TOOLS OF THE TRADE

Binoculars are standard equipment for wildlife watchers and are indispensable for seeing and identifying animals in the field. The most popular models magnify the subject 7 or 8 times and are lightweight, weather resistant, and moderately priced. There are many variations on the traditional design, including compact models that fit easily into a fanny pack or belt pouch and large binoculars with greater light-gathering capability for viewing in low light conditions. Check with an optics dealer for advice on a pair that will meet your needs.

A **spotting scope** and tripod will extend your viewing range considerably. Scopes typically magnify an image from 20 to 60 times and can have fixed or zoom magnification lenses. Once wildlife has been located with binoculars it's often possible to find the subject with a scope for a better view. Practice with fairly stationary objects, such as a perched hawk or wading heron, before trying to follow and focus on a running deer or flying duck.

There are a wide variety of **field guides** available to help you identify the wildlife and wild plants you encounter. Many have drawings and photographs which point out an animal's distinctive features, colors, or patterns, called field marks, which greatly aid in identification. You'll find birds, butterflies, wildflowers, and even whales in field guides.

Wildlife **photography** and **videography** is growing in popularity almost as fast as wildlife watching. Preserving wildlife memories on film is a satisfying hobby that adds to the enjoyment of the viewing experience. Equipment is a matter of personal preference, not to mention personal finance. Still photographers using 35 mm cameras and telephoto lenses have a host of options. Camcorders with 10- or 12-power zoom features are popular with videographers. The best times for photography are often early and late in the day, when the rich, golden light produces dramatic shadows and increased color contrast. Show animals exhibiting natural behavior in their natural surroundings by keeping distance between the subject and the camera. If you approach too closely, the bird or animal may flee, spoiling the viewing and photo opportunity for yourself and others.

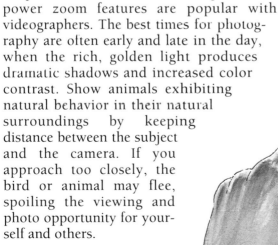

WILDLIFE VIEWING TIPS

There are several different ways to watch wildlife. One of the simplest is to **use your car** as a portable blind while driving through areas where vehicles are permitted. When you see an animal, such as a wild turkey at the edge of a field or a cedar waxwing feeding in a mountain ash, pull safely off the road and sit tight. Wildlife will often tolerate vehicles but perceive a person on foot as a threat. A window mount for a spotting scope can be a useful item under these viewing conditions.

Another effective viewing method is to hike into an area and find a spot that offers a good vantage. Places where different habitat types meet, the edge of a beaver pond for example, can be particularly good. **Sit quietly**, using the available brush and vegetation to break up your outline, and slowly turn your head and move your eyes to scan the area before you. Take a lesson from hawks and owls, who are by necessity among the most efficient wildlife watchers around. These birds routinely sit motionless and survey their surroundings for hours, watching and listening for the slightest movements and sounds. Their survival depends on being able to detect the presence of other animals,

any of which may be a potential meal. The flight of a butterfly, the twitching of a deer's tail, or the call of a songbird will catch your eye or ear. Carefully raise your binoculars, zero in on the source, and enjoy.

Walking through an area helps you learn about habitat, trail systems, waterways, and wildlife movements. Go slowly, pausing often to scan and listen. Look for tracks, droppings, gnawings, and other indications that wildlife is near. When something gets your attention, stop, focus on the spot, and slowly raise your binoculars to your eyes.

Wildlife activity picks up in the **early morning and late evening** hours. Getting up a little earlier or staying in the field a little later can be worth the effort. **Weather** can also influence animal activity. Calm periods before a winter snowstorm or just after a heavy downpour can be productive for viewing wildlife.

Don't overlook the more **common and conspicuous wildlife** you encounter. The behavior of a Canada goose or eastern chipmunk can be as interesting as that of a coyote. There's also a **micro-world** of wildlife all around. Study a dragonfly, ladybug, or ant colony in the comfort of your own backyard. All of their colors and movements serve a purpose in their daily interactions.

LOOKING IN THE RIGHT PLACE AT THE RIGHT TIME

Wildlife depends on its **habitat** for survival. Many species in Massachusetts are found only in very limited habitats, such as common terns on barrier beaches or bald eagles on major water bodies. Other species, like raccoons, white-tailed deer, and black-capped chickadees, can exploit habitats ranging from deep woods to suburban backyards. Knowing the habitat an animal uses and where that habitat is found is the first step in successful wildlife viewing. Recognizing this link between wildlife and its habitat is also a fundamental lesson in conservation. If animals don't have an area that provides the needed combination of food, water, and cover, they cannot survive there.

Daily and seasonal timing is also a critical factor when looking for wildlife. Red-tailed hawks, song sparrows, and chipmunks are only active during the day. Great horned owls, little brown bats, and

opossums are most active at night. Choose your viewing times based on the wildlife you hope to encounter. Wildlife are active seasonally as well. Painted turtles and bullfrogs emerge from winter dormancy shortly after red-winged blackbirds return on their spring migration. These animals remain active throughout the warmer months only to disappear again with the onset of winter. The colder weather brings wintering blue jays, juncos, pine siskins, and evening grosbeaks to forests and feeders. Set your viewing schedule to match the changing seasons.

Migration is an exciting time for wildlife watchers. Catching the peak of the fall hawk flight or being surrounded by brightly colored spring warblers provide sights and sounds not soon forgotten. Consult field guides and join a local bird or nature club to learn more about prime times and places to witness migrations.

BIODIVERSITY—OUR COMMON WEALTH

Nature is frequently referred to as a "Web of Life," with all the living parts of the natural world connected directly or indirectly through an intricate network resembling a spider web. Forming the web is an array of unique ecosystems and wildlife communities composed of plants, invertebrates, reptiles, amphibians, fish, birds, mammals, and the habitat elements that sustain them.

Think of each species as an individual strand of the web. The intersections of the strands can be thought of as natural communities where species overlap and are interdependent. Each intersection represents a unique community—such as a freshwater wetland, a grassland, or a barrier beach—upon which particular groups of species rely for survival. The greater the number of strands or species, the greater the number of intersections or communities; the greater the number of

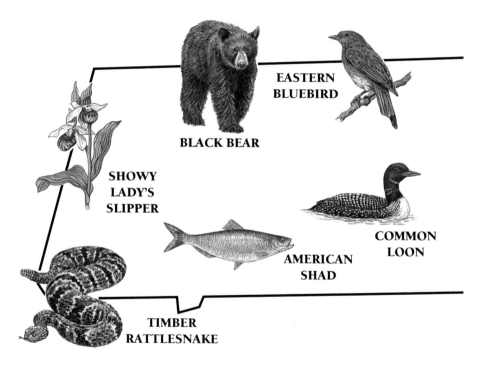

EASTERN BLUEBIRD

BLACK BEAR

SHOWY LADY'S SLIPPER

COMMON LOON

AMERICAN SHAD

TIMBER RATTLESNAKE

intersections, the stronger the web or, for this example, the healthier the environment.

This diversity of biological features, from the simplest single-celled organism to the most complex ecosystem, is collectively known as "biodiversity," and it is critically important to the health of the environment. In simplest terms, biodiversity is the variety of species and habitats and the connections between them that are necessary to make natural systems function.

Picture the habitat needs of the species shown on the map. How many species can you associate with a particular habitat? Which ones share similar habitat? How many have very specific habitat needs, and how many would seem completely out of place elsewhere on the map?

To take the web analogy one step further, envision breaking strands as species are lost to extinction. With each lost strand, intersections weaken as natural communities change and fail. Ultimately, with the loss of many systems, the entire web collapses. Thus, to preserve the health and viability of the environment, we must conserve the biodiversity of that environment.

In Massachusetts we share a "common wealth" of wildlife resources that are critical to our own web. While watching and learning about the species, take a moment to consider and appreciate their place, and yours, in the natural world. Ask "how" and "why" species interact, taking note of the importance of the habitats on which those species depend. You'll soon agree that biodiversity is both worth watching and worth conserving.

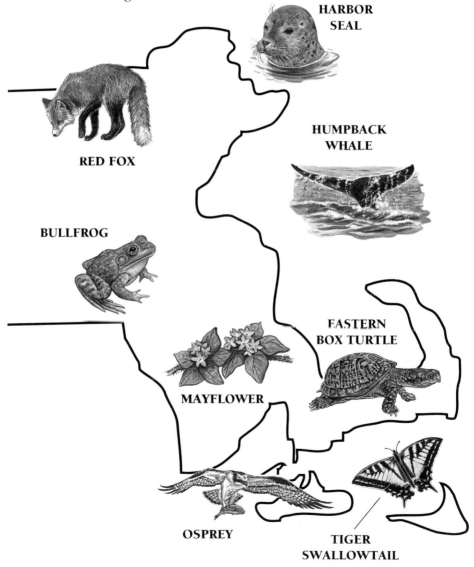

HARBOR SEAL

RED FOX

HUMPBACK WHALE

BULLFROG

EASTERN BOX TURTLE

MAYFLOWER

OSPREY

TIGER SWALLOWTAIL

Wildlife is constantly moving. From local movements relating to daily feeding and resting behavior to seasonal migrations for breeding and wintering, many species found in Massachusetts travel over much of the Western Hemisphere. A look at a few representative species will shed some light on when, where, and why wildlife engages in "Mass." Migrations.

Broad-winged and **sharp-shinned hawks** breed in wooded areas throughout much of northern and eastern North America, including Massachusetts. As winter approaches, broad-wings must travel to Central and South America to find rodents, amphibians, and snakes, while sharp-shins spread out across southern North America and Mexico in pursuit of flocks of songbirds. Mid-September is prime time to view the annual hawk migration from many Massachusetts summits, when tens of thousands of hawks ride thermal currents and updrafts in groups known as "kettles" over the Berkshires, Holyoke Range, Wachusett Mountain, and the Blue Hills.

Atlantic salmon are being restored to the Connecticut and Merrimack River drainages through an ambitious public and private partnership. Young salmon, raised in hatcheries, are stocked in tributaries before descending the rivers to the ocean. Remaining in the north Atlantic until mature, the adult salmon then return to fresh water to spawn. Natural spawning has been observed in the Westfield River, showing promise for the future of the project. Salmon can be observed ascending the Connecticut River in May and June at the Barrett Fishway in Holyoke and the Turner's Falls Fish Ladder in Montague.

Red bats are one of nine species of bats known in Massachusetts. Rather than hibernate in caves, mines, or buildings, as little brown bats and other species do, red bats remain active and migrate in the fall and spring. They alternately fly across their range from southern Canada and the eastern United States to the Gulf Coast, seeking areas where insects are seasonally abundant. Red bats are known to migrate in loose flocks resembling birds and can be seen leaving tree roosts well before dusk.

Right whales engage in an oceanic migration that is currently being studied. Understanding the timing and movements of these critically endangered mammals is important in minimizing collisions between whales and ships. Such accidents are the leading cause of right whale mortality. After summering in northern waters, pregnant females move south to calving grounds off the Georgia and Florida coast. The wintering movements of adult males and other members of the population remain largely unknown.

Monarch butterflies are among the most common and easily recognized butterflies. Their fall migration takes them from their summer range of south-central Canada and the continental United States to wintering destinations in mountainous regions of Mexico. September and October are usually the best months for watching monarchs on the wing. Swarms of hundreds to thousands can occur during the south-

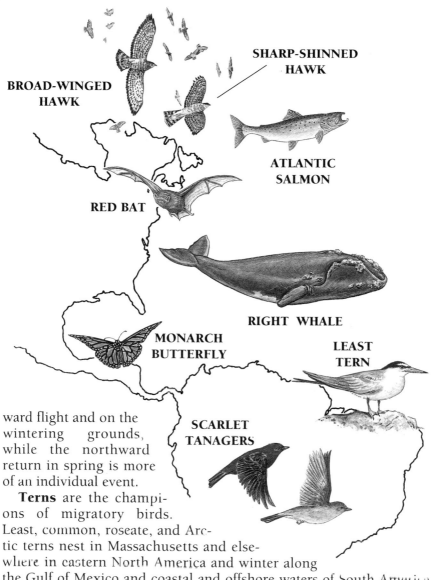

BROAD-WINGED HAWK

SHARP-SHINNED HAWK

ATLANTIC SALMON

RED BAT

RIGHT WHALE

MONARCH BUTTERFLY

LEAST TERN

SCARLET TANAGERS

ward flight and on the wintering grounds, while the northward return in spring is more of an individual event.

Terns are the champions of migratory birds. Least, common, roseate, and Arctic terns nest in Massachusetts and elsewhere in eastern North America and winter along the Gulf of Mexico and coastal and offshore waters of South America. Arctic terns, which nest from Massachusetts to extreme northern Canada, are known to winter at sea in the subantarctic off Argentina, making their 22,000-mile round trip migration the longest of any bird.

Scarlet tanagers belong to a group of more than 100 species of birds collectively known as "neotropical migrants," those that breed in temperate North America and winter in the new-world, or "neo," tropics of South America, the Caribbean, and Mexico. In Massachusetts, tanagers are found in large tracts of mixed forest where they nest and forage in the canopy. To address the many issues of neotropical migrant conservation, including nesting and wintering habitat protection, an international coalition of conservationists has formed "Partners in Flight." Through "Partners," protection strategies can be formed that transcend the political boundaries over which the migrant birds freely range.

MASSACHUSETTS
WILDLIFE VIEWING AREAS

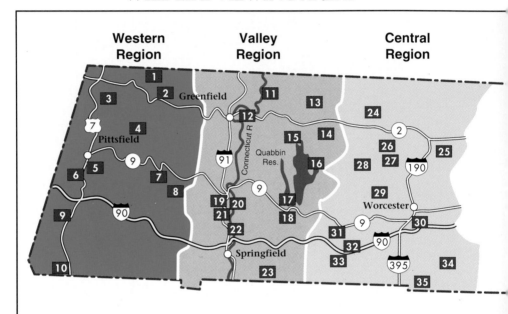

Western Region

Valley Region

Central Region

Greenfield
Pittsfield
Connecticut R.
Quabbin Res.
Springfield
Worcester

WILDLIFE VIEWING AREA

Highway Signs
As you travel in Massachusetts and other states, look for these signs on highways and other roads. They identify the route to follow to reach wildlife viewing sites.

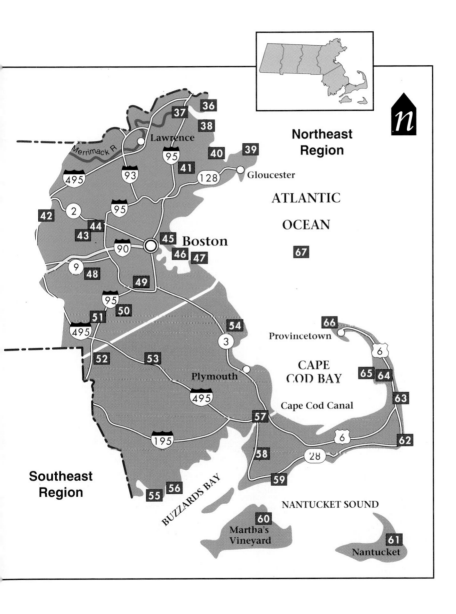

Northeast
Region

ATLANTIC

OCEAN

Boston

Gloucester

Lawrence

Merrimack R.

CAPE
COD BAY

Provincetown

Cape Cod Canal

Plymouth

Southeast
Region

BUZZARDS BAY

NANTUCKET SOUND

Martha's
Vineyard

Nantucket

WESTERN REGION—BERKSHIRE HILLS

The Berkshire Hills represent the Massachusetts section of the Appalachian Mountains. Rising from the Connecticut River Valley to the east and peaking at the summit of Mount Greylock, the region is bordered on three sides by the states of Vermont, New York, and Connecticut. The Deerfield, Westfield, and Housatonic rivers drain the hillsides and are fed by many clear, fast-running streams. The Appalachian Trail winds its way through the forests and along the ridgetops with many access points and breathtaking vistas along the way Ten wildlife viewing sites are scattered across the region, offering the solitude of old-growth forest, the scenery of a mountaintop, and the songs of nesting birds.

Monument Mountain (Site 9) rises in stark contrast to the surrounding Berkshire Hills. The jagged rock face was once a nesting site for peregrine falcons. In 1850, American authors Herman Melville and Nathaniel Hawthorne met for the first time at the summit. BILL BYRNE

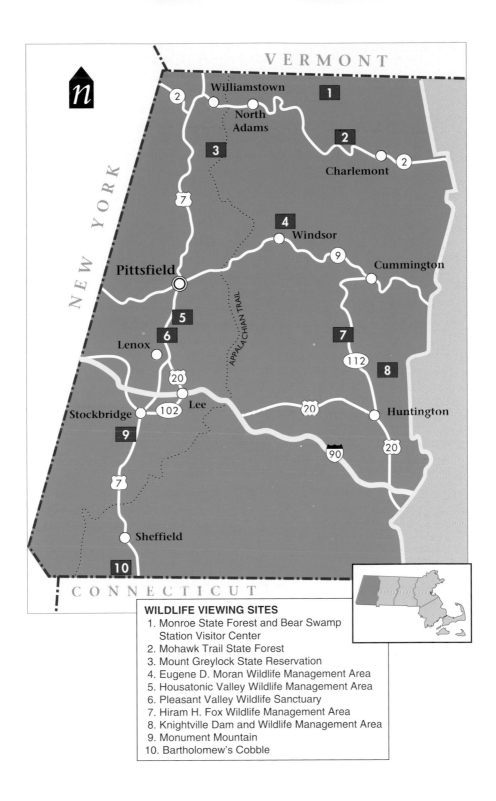

VERMONT

NEW YORK

CONNECTICUT

1 Williamstown
North Adams
1
2
2 Charlemont
3
7
4 Windsor
9 Cummington
Pittsfield
5
6
Lenox
7
112
8
20
Lee
20 Huntington
Stockbridge 102
90 20
9
7
Sheffield
10

APPALACHIAN TRAIL

WILDLIFE VIEWING SITES
1. Monroe State Forest and Bear Swamp
   Station Visitor Center
2. Mohawk Trail State Forest
3. Mount Greylock State Reservation
4. Eugene D. Moran Wildlife Management Area
5. Housatonic Valley Wildlife Management Area
6. Pleasant Valley Wildlife Sanctuary
7. Hiram H. Fox Wildlife Management Area
8. Knightville Dam and Wildlife Management Area
9. Monument Mountain
10. Bartholomew's Cobble

27

1. MONROE STATE FOREST AND BEAR SWAMP STATION VISITOR CENTER

Description: Time and technology meet on the steep slopes of the northern Berkshires, where old-growth forest exists adjacent to a hydroelectric generating facility. Experience the solitude and beauty of the forest in the Dunbar Brook Backcountry Area and learn about the natural and technological resources of the site at the Bear Swamp Visitor Center.

Viewing Information: From the visitor center parking lot, use binoculars to scan the opposite hillside for white-tailed deer or black bears foraging at the power line right-of-way. Check the ridgetop for soaring birds of prey and ravens. Obtain a map at the center and inquire about recent wildlife sightings, then proceed to the Dunbar Brook Trail parking area. Follow the trail along the boulder-strewn brook, listening and looking for great-crested and acadian flycatchers. About 1 mile from the parking lot, the trail emerges from dense hemlocks. Note the change in the composition of the forest, the more open appearance, the downed tree trunks and new tree sprouts. An absence of stumps, stone walls, or other signs of a past human presence suggests that this area was never cut for timber or cleared for agriculture. Core samples from select sugar maple and hemlock confirm that these trees are more than 200 years old, while a single black birch is estimated at more than 300 years. These trees are among the oldest to be found anywhere in the state, and they form a 10-acre block of old-growth forest.

Directions: *Follow Route 2 west through the center of Charlemont to a right turn on Zoar Road just before crossing the Deerfield River. Follow Zoar Road as it parallels the Deerfield, bearing left under the railroad bridge at the intersection with Rowe Road. Zoar Road becomes River Road at the town line. Stay on River Road for the 7-mile drive up the Deerfield Valley to the Bear Swamp Station Visitor Center on the right. The Dunbar Brook Trail is 1 mile past the center on the left.*

Ownership: DEM (413) 339-5504; New England Power (508) 366-9011

Size: 4,320 acres   **Closest Town:** Charlemont

Wildlife watching can be an everyday activity because wildlife is all around us. Take a closer look around your home, workplace, local park, or conservation area. You'll be surprised by what's there.

2. MOHAWK TRAIL STATE FOREST

Description: Named for the Native Americans who inhabited the region, this forested tract offers a chance to see large mammals and their sign. It also contains five stands of old-growth timber and seasonally provides on-site camping and interpretive programs. The Mohawk Trail (Route 2) is a scenic drive at any time of year but is most popular in October, when fall foliage is at its peak.

Viewing Information: From the state forest headquarters, take the Indian Trail toward Clark Mountain. Check stands of beech trees for black bear claw marks in the smooth bark and look for broken branches and disturbed leaf litter on the forest floor, evidence that bears have been feeding. Watch for buck rubs on small-diameter saplings, places where the bark has been rubbed off by male white-tailed deer jousting with their antlers in anticipation of the November breeding season. Also look for ragged tips on sprouting woody vegetation and low hemlock branches, particularly on south-facing slopes. This suggests deer feeding activity in the winter. The nature trail at the east end of the campground is another good viewing area. While driving the Mohawk Trail, scan roadside fields and dairy farm pastures for flocks of wild turkeys, and be sure to stop and sample some of the many maple sugar products for which the area is renowned.

Directions: *From Interstate 91, take Route 2 west for 24 miles to the entrance.*

Ownership: DEM (413) 339-5504

Size: 6,450 acres   **Closest Town:** Charlemont

Black bears are becoming increasingly common in western Massachusetts. The population now numbers more than 1,000 animals. BILL BYRNE

3. MOUNT GREYLOCK STATE RESERVATION

Description: Stand atop the Commonwealth's highest peak, 3,491-foot Mount Greylock, and take in the panoramic five-state view. The Appalachian Trail connnects Greylock with Mounts Fitch and Williams to the north and Saddle Ball Mountain to the south. Steep-sided ravines are created by Hopper and Money Brooks, providing sheltered riparian habitat.

Viewing Information: The Mount Greylock Visitor Center introduces viewers to many options for experiencing the ridges and glens of the reservation. Except when snow forces road closures, a drive to the summit is possible. Multiple hiking trails of varying difficulty are available. In June, check the subalpine habitat near the summit, looking and listening for blackpoll warblers and golden-crowned kinglets. Thrushes and waxwings can be seen among the mountain ash. At lower elevations, be alert for northern goshawks; watch for flashes of gray as they maneuver low through the forest in pursuit of ruffed grouse or blue jays. Field edges frequently conceal white-tailed deer, and signs of black bears can be found on hardwood slopes.

Directions: From Route 2 in Williamstown, follow Route 7 south through New Ashford. Watch for Mount Greylock State Reservation signs on the left. From Massachusetts Turnpike (Interstate 90), take exit 2 to Route 20. Follow Route 20 west to Route 7. Take Route 7 north through Pittsfield and Lanesboro. Look for reservation signs on the right.

Ownership: DEM (413) 499-4262

Size: 12,500 acres   **Closest Town:** Williamstown

4. EUGENE D. MORAN WILDLIFE MANAGEMENT AREA

Description: Old fields, mixed northern hardwoods, softwood plantations, alder swamps, and wet sedge meadows give a diverse character to this area. With an average elevation of 2,000 feet, many scenic vistas of the surrounding Berkshires are available.

Viewing Information: On the eastern side of Route 8A, Fobes Hill rises gradually to a rounded summit, an uncrowded vantage where migrating hawks are frequently seen in September. More than 182 bird species have been identified on the property, including 27 species of warblers. Mammals present include white-tailed deer, black bears, fishers, and bobcats. Check for otter sign along Windsor Brook and the edges of beaver ponds.

Directions: From Route 9 in Windsor, follow Route 8A north for approximately 1 mile to parking areas on either side of the road.

Ownership: DFW (413) 447-9789

Size: 1,147 acres   **Closest Town:** Windsor

Description: The Housatonic River winds and wanders over the flat flood-plain, through forests, along fields, and into quiet backwaters. One-third of the area is wetland, so the best way to experience the site is by canoe. From the river, the valley rises gradually to the west and abruptly to the east, making the waterway a natural travel corridor for wildlife.

Viewing Information: Paddling or drifting a canoe over still waters is a great way to watch wildlife along the Housatonic. This area is most noted for its bird populations, with more than 170 species known to occur. Wetlands-dependent birds like soras and Virginia rails are common. Muskrats can be seen swimming along the riverbank or feeding on aquatic plants. Fields adjacent to the river are favored by woodcock for springtime courtship flights. Encroaching brush shelters cottontail rabbits. Ruffed grouse prefer the surrounding forest and are quick to flush from cover when approached. Listen for the deep-toned whirl of their wings as they explode into flight.

Directions: *From the Massachusetts Turnpike (Interstate 90), take exit 2 in Lee and follow Route 20 west to the merge with Route 7. Stay on routes 20 and 7 for approximately 4.5 miles to a right turn on New Lenox Road. Follow New Lenox Road to the railroad crossing. The first parking area is on the left just beyond the railroad crossing. Additional parking and a canoe launch site are 1,500 feet farther on the right.*

Ownership: DFW (413) 447-9789

Size: 818 acres   **Closest City:** Pittsfield

The American woodcock uses its long beak to probe soft soils for earthworms. Its protective coloration makes this ground-dwelling bird difficult to spot. Listen for its springtime "peent" call at dawn and dusk.
BILL BYRNE

WESTERN

6. PLEASANT VALLEY WILDLIFE SANCTUARY

Description: Seeps and brooks have carved small valleys in the surrounding forested hillsides. Beavers have dammed the drainages, creating a series of ponds and wet meadows where wildlife thrives. The visitor center is staffed with knowledgeable naturalists who give interpretive programs—a great way to learn about the site.

Viewing Information: Dawn and dusk are premier times for viewing beavers. Watch for these large rodents stripping bark, felling trees, or repairing lodges and dams. When beavers aren't evident, check the pond margins for fresh cuttings. Chisel-like tooth marks from the beavers' incisors will be visible on the pointed stumps, and wood chips will litter the ground. Piles of mud and leaves near the water are scent mounds made by beavers to mark territory. In fall, look for large amounts of brushy vegetation stockpiled under water at the lodge entrances. The beaver colonies use these winter "caches" for food when ice covers the pond. Other animals to look for include tree swallows, red-shouldered hawks, and minks. The sanctuary is closed Mondays.

Directions: *From the Massachusetts Turnpike (Interstate 90), take exit 2 in Lee and travel north on routes 7 and 20 for 6.6 miles. Turn left on West Dugway Road. Follow signs to the site entrance.*

Ownership: MAS (413) 637-0320

Size: 1,153 acres   **Closest Town:** Lenox

An adult and a kit beaver feed on a freshly cut maple sapling. These individuals are members of one of several family groups found in the Pleasant Valley Wildlife Sanctuary. BILL BYRNE

7. HIRAM H. FOX WILDLIFE MANAGEMENT AREA

Description: This remote site consists of two connected parcels featuring roll-ing, forested hills, ledge outcrops, wetlands, and the Little River. To improve wildlife habitat, 1- to 5-acre forest openings and thinnings have been created using cutting and controlled burning. An annual breeding bird survey moni-tors the numbers and species composition of nesting migratory land birds.

Viewing Information: The steeper eastern parcel includes a section of the Little River, a stocked trout stream. The hemlock and hardwood slopes are fa-vored by white-tailed deer and black bears. The gently rolling western parcel features clearings maintained with controlled fires. Mourning warblers are found here. Breeding birds regularly heard include American redstarts and winter wrens. Lines of numbered posts identify survey transects, the routes bi-ologists follow to record data on nesting birds. A wetland forms the headwa-ters of Moss Meadow Brook, an excellent area for red-shouldered hawks.

Directions: *From Route 9 in Cummington, take Route 112 south through Worthington Corners and Worthington. Approximately 4 miles beyond the center of Worthington, turn right on Goss Hill Road and follow it for 1 mile to the parking area on the right.*

Ownership: DFW (413) 447-9789

Size: 2,553 acres   **Closest Town:** Worthington

WESTERN

8. KNIGHTVILLE DAM AND WILDLIFE MANAGEMENT AREA

Description: The flood-control basin at Knightville encompasses extensive forested tracts of white pine, hemlock, and oak mixed with more than 200 acres of open fields, marshes, and watercourses.

Viewing Information: Soaring birds like red-tailed and red-shouldered hawks and ravens can be seen from the dam. In forested sections and near field mar-gins, ruffed grouse can be heard drumming and wild turkeys gobble and dis-play in spring. The fields also host extensive wildflower blooms that attract a variety of butterflies. The Claude M. Hill Horse Trail and a network of cart roads provide access to the Westfield River and tributaries.

Directions: *From the Massachusetts Turnpike (Interstate 90), take exit 3 at Westfield and follow Route 20 west to Huntington. From Huntington, take Route 112 north for 4 miles to Knightville Dam Road on the right.*

Ownership: USACE (413) 667-3430

Size: 2,430 acres   **Closest Town:** Huntington

9. MONUMENT MOUNTAIN

Description: From a distance, the exposed quartzite rock that forms the heart of Monument Mountain appears white against the background of forest and sky. The forces of nature have chiseled away at the mountain, producing a talus slope of boulders on its eastern side. Tall white pines and oaks flank the outcrops and shelter an understory of striped maple, young chestnut, and mountain laurel.

Viewing Information: Three miles of trails, with varying degrees of steepness, make their way past massive boulders and barren outcrops to the top of the mountain. The summit affords striking views of the surrounding Berkshire ridges and valleys. The cliffs are home to nesting common ravens that often can be seen and heard as they soar on updrafts produced by wind deflected up the sheer sides of the mountain. Turkey vultures are three-season residents, drifting south in late fall with thousands of migrating broad-winged and sharp-shinned hawks.

Directions: From the Massachusetts Turnpike (Interstate 90), take exit 2 in Lee and travel west on Route 102. From the intersection of routes 102 and 7 in Stockbridge, take Route 7 south for 3 miles to the parking area on the right.

Ownership: TTOR (413) 298-3239

Size: 503 acres   **Closest Town:** Stockbridge

Common ravens first nested in Massachusetts in the early 1980s and are now found in association with most large cliffs in the central and western part of the state. These raven chicks show their bright pink mouth linings in anticipation of a meal.
BILL BYRNE

10. BARTHOLOMEW'S COBBLE

Description: At the southern extreme of Massachusetts' Berkshire Mountains, marble and granite outcrops form an intricate landscape—a "cobble" of boulders and ledge. The soils produced by the eroding rock support more than 740 species of plants. These plants provide food and shelter for an abundance of wildlife, including more than 240 species of birds.

Viewing Information: Springtime blooms of trillium and columbine give way to ostrich and cinnamon ferns in summer. Fall brings profusions of goldenrod and aster. Bobolinks and bluebirds can be seen in and around Ashley Field on the trail to Hurlburt's Hill, an excellent fall hawk-watching vantage and scenic overlook of the Housatonic River Valley. White-tailed deer are commonly found in Ashley Field, particularly early and late in the day. Trails meander along the river and through beech/maple woodlands. A companion booklet available on site describes the 0.5-mile Ledges Trail and the cobble's natural history.

Directions: *From the Massachusetts Turnpike (Interstate 90), take exit 2 for Route 102 in Lee. Follow Route 102 west to Route 7 south in Stockbridge. Take Route 7 south to Sheffield. Continue on Route 7 south for 1.6 miles past the center of Sheffield. Turn right on Route 7A and follow it for 0.5 mile to Rannapo Road on the right. Go 1.5 miles on Rannapo Road and turn right on Weatogue Road. The entrance and parking area are on the left.*

Ownership: TTOR (413) 229-8600

Size: 275 acres   **Closest Town:** Sheffield

Columbine is one of the hundreds of plant species found at Bartholomew's Cobble. With a field guide and a magnifying glass, a wildlife watcher can identify a variety of plants and wildflowers during a single visit.
BILL BYRNE

VALLEY REGION—CONNECTICUT AND SWIFT RIVER VALLEYS

The Connecticut River Valley cuts through the region from Vermont to Connecticut. This broad, flat valley is home to agricultural fields and flood-plain forests, and is intersected abruptly by the Holyoke Range, a ridge that runs east/west, rather than north/south. In contrast, the Swift River Valley is characterized by a series of rolling ridges, a feature that made the area suitable for damming and flooding in the 1920s. The result is the 39-square-mile Quabbin Reservoir, which today supplies drinking water to 2.5 million Massachusetts residents. There are 13 wildlife viewing sites in the region, where you might encounter anything from bald eagles to beavers, mergansers to moose, or turkey vultures to trout.

The Connecticut River flows south toward the Holyoke Range. The Holyoke Range is a favorite hawk-watching area with Skinner State Park (Site 20) and Mount Tom State Reservation (Site 21) providing premier viewing sites. BILL BYRNE

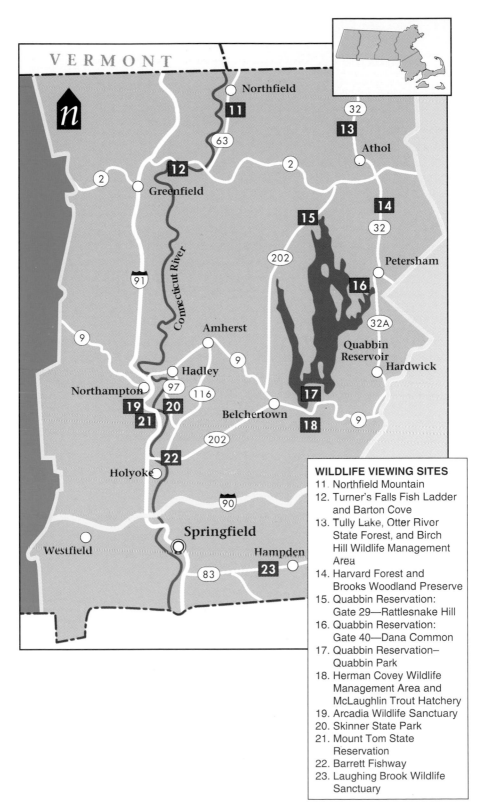

VERMONT

Northfield

11

63

12

Greenfield

2

13

32

Athol

2

14

32

15

202

Petersham

91

Connecticut River

16

9

Amherst

9

32A

Hadley

97

116

Quabbin
Reservoir

Hardwick

Northampton

19 **20**

21

Belchertown

17

18

9

202

22

Holyoke

90

Springfield

Westfield

Hampden

83

23

WILDLIFE VIEWING SITES

11. Northfield Mountain
12. Turner's Falls Fish Ladder and Barton Cove
13. Tully Lake, Otter River State Forest, and Birch Hill Wildlife Management Area
14. Harvard Forest and Brooks Woodland Preserve
15. Quabbin Reservation: Gate 29—Rattlesnake Hill
16. Quabbin Reservation: Gate 40—Dana Common
17. Quabbin Reservation–Quabbin Park
18. Herman Covey Wildlife Management Area and McLaughlin Trout Hatchery
19. Arcadia Wildlife Sanctuary
20. Skinner State Park
21. Mount Tom State Reservation
22. Barrett Fishway
23. Laughing Brook Wildlife Sanctuary

11. NORTHFIELD MOUNTAIN

Description: The Northfield Mountain Recreation and Environmental Center combines a diversity of wildlife habitat with a well-staffed facility. Woodlands, wetlands, and open fields are joined by a network of marked trails. The Connecticut River is accessible via a guided riverboat tour.

Viewing Information: Begin at the visitor center at the base of Northfield Mountain to plan a route for a hike, mountain bike trip, or cross-country ski tour on any of the 25 miles of trails. Follow the 1-mile nature trail that features upland, wetland, forest, and open habitats, with information on the geology of the mountain. Watch for pileated woodpeckers and their distinctive rectangular cuttings in the trees of the mixed forest. Trail edges are good places to check for tracks of white-tailed deer, eastern coyotes, or bobcats. Both the maintained and overgrown fields are favorite places of wild turkeys, bluebirds, and red foxes. Watch the ridgeline for soaring turkey vultures or explore a well-used porcupine trail along rocky outcrops. (Porcupines create defined trails between denning and feeding sites.) On the 1.5-hour riverboat tour, visitors often see waterfowl, kingfishers, and bank swallows. Bald eagles often make an appearance where the riverboat enters Barton Cove. Call ahead for the riverboat schedule and trail conditions. Information on exhibits, bus tours, and programs describing the natural, cultural, historic, and economic features of the area is available at the visitor center.

Directions: *From Route 2, follow Route 63 north for 2 miles to the visitor center entrance on the right.*

Ownership: NU (413) 659-3714

Size: 2,500 acres   **Closest Town:** Northfield

A young red fox is caught yawning near its den in the early morning light. The fox is wet with dew after hunting insects in the tall grasses.
BILL BYRNE

38

Description: The Turner's Falls Dam presents a major obstacle to some 40,000 fish ascending the Connecticut River to spawn. The Turner's Falls fish ladders enable fish to pass around the dam by following a gently sloped series of submerged steps. At the top of the ladder the fish pass viewing windows before entering the calm waters of Barton Cove. Barton Cove is a shallow backwater created by the dam and is rich in aquatic life. Upstream from the dam a mile-long peninsula offers a hiking trail, access to vantage points, and a seasonal campground.

Viewing Information: The fish ladder is open to the public Wednesday through Sunday, 9 A.M. to 5 P.M., during the May and June fish migration. Call for current information. American shad, blueback herring, sea lamprey, and Atlantic salmon may be seen from viewing windows. Views of Barton Cove are available from the fish ladder and Unity Park on the south side of the river as well as from the state boat ramp and Barton Cove campground on the north and east side. The cove is a popular waterfowl resting and feeding area in spring and fall. Diving ducks such as hooded mergansers, common goldeneyes, and ring-necks are joined by dabbling ducks like green-winged teal, black ducks, mallards, and pintails. A resident pair of adult bald eagles are frequently visible from April through August. Young eagles may be seen and heard in late summer. I like the campground trail past an abandoned dinosaur track quarry and enjoy the water view from the rim of a rock-sided plunge pool.

Directions: *From Interstate 91, take Route 2 east. At the second set of traffic lights, located at Route 2 and the Turner's Falls Bridge, turn right and cross the bridge on Avenue A. Just over the bridge, turn left on 1st Street. Parking is on the left. The state boat ramp is 0.5 mile east of the Route 2 traffic lights, and the campground entrance is 0.7 mile east.*

Ownership: NU (413) 659-3714

Size: 500 acres   **Closest Town:** Montague

Add a large, plastic trash bag to your list of wildlife watching equipment. Cut a hole in the bottom and the bag can serve as a handy rain poncho. Otherwise, pack out your own trash and pick up any extra you find along the trail.

VALLEY

13. TULLY LAKE, OTTER RIVER STATE FOREST, AND BIRCH HILL WILDLIFE MANAGEMENT AREA

Description: Multiple state and federal agencies combine to protect more than 20,000 acres of lakes, rivers, wetlands, and uplands offering an array of wildlife viewing and recreational options.

Viewing Information: Tully Lake and secluded Long Pond are prime sites for viewing ravens, minks, wood ducks, and tree swallows via hiking trails or canoe. The nearby Birch Hill Wildlife Management Area and adjacent Otter River State Forest and Lake Dennison Recreation Area are home to beavers, gray foxes, fishers, and a growing moose population.

Directions: *From Route 2, follow Route 32 north to Athol. Continue for 3.5 miles beyond Athol to the Tully Lake office on the left. For Birch Hill, Otter River, and Lake Dennison, take Route 2 to exit 20 for Baldwinville Road. Follow Baldwinville Road north to Route 202 in Baldwinville. Follow Route 202 north through Baldwinville to respective site entrances on left.*

Ownership: Tully Lake, USACE (508) 249-2547; Otter River & Lake Dennison, DEM (508) 939-8962; Birch Hill WMA, DFW (508) 939-8977

Size: 20,000+ acres   **Closest Towns:** Athol & Winchendon

A female, or cow, moose pauses while feeding in a forest opening. Dark brown hair makes these largest members of the deer family difficult to spot in shadows or at night.
BILL BYRNE

40

14. HARVARD FOREST AND BROOKS WOODLAND PRESERVE

Description: The Fisher Museum at Harvard Forest features 23 natural history dioramas depicting the land-use practices and forest ecology of the region. The forest's Prospect Hill Tract contains two short interpretive nature trails, 15 miles of unmarked trails and cart roads, and a fire tower that affords a view of Wachusett Mountain to the east and New Hampshire's Mount Monadnock to the north. Nearby, the Brooks Woodland Preserve encompasses both the Roaring Brook and Swift River tracts, where hemlock, white pine, red oak, and shagbark hickory dominate the hillsides. At Roaring Brook, a 10-acre marsh is central among the habitats. The clear-running East Branch of the Swift River is a scenic ribbon and wildlife travel corridor winding through the Swift River Tract.

Viewing Information: The history of the central Massachusetts forests from the time of the native Nipmucks through the present is traced by the Fisher Museum exhibits. Maps of the Prospect Hill Tract are available. A hike to the fire tower may reveal red-eyed and solitary vireos, eastern wood pewees, black-throated blue warblers, and red-breasted nuthatches. From the tower, scan the treetops and skyline for rose-breasted grosbeaks, scarlet tanagers, and soaring broad-winged hawks. For a different habitat, drive to the Roaring Brook and Swift River tracts and watch the marsh edges for song sparrows, muskrats, and minks. The waters of the Swift River shelter colorful native brook trout, which can be seen taking insects from the surface.

Directions: *From Route 2, travel 3 miles south on Route 32 to the Harvard Forest/ Fisher Museum/Prospect Hill entrance on the left. From the museum, travel 3 miles south to Petersham, turn left on East Street, and proceed 0.8 mile to the Roaring Brook property on the left. To reach the Swift River Tract from Petersham, travel south on Route 32 to a stop sign at the junction with Route 122. Turn left on routes 32/122 and travel 1.5 miles south. Turn left on Quaker Drive. Entrances are on both sides of the road just after the Swift River bridge.*

Ownership: Harvard University & TTOR (508) 724-3302

Size: 1,510 combined acres   **Closest Town:** Petersham

Some official state symbols of Massachusetts include the black-capped chickadee as state bird, ladybug as state insect, mayflower as state flower, and American elm as state tree.

15. QUABBIN RESERVATION: GATE 29—RATTLESNAKE HILL

Description: Gate 29 allows access to a variety of habitats at the northern end of Quabbin Reservoir. The road in places is lined with stately sugar maples and passes through abandoned fields and orchards, hinting at the recent human presence. A power line right-of-way provides a large opening in the forest where woody plants and shrubs sprout. The paved road, where bicycles are permitted, skirts the north and west sides of Rattlesnake Hill through dark stands of white pine and hemlock before ending abruptly at the waters of the reservoir.

Viewing Information: Numbered posts identify an interpretive walk along the first part of the 2.5-mile road. Obtain a companion brochure with descriptions of each site from the MDC Forestry Office directly across Route 202 from the gate. Listen for yellow-rumped and Canada warblers singing from the trees and the distinctive "drink-your-tea" call of the eastern towhee coming from the brushy understory. At the power line, American kestrels and red-tailed and red-shouldered hawks can be seen soaring or perched on transmission towers. The paved road bears to the right through a dense pine stand where black-capped chickadees and white-breasted nuthatches are found. The road then emerges toward the shoreline. From water's edge, common loons and Canada geese can be seen, and bald eagles soar overhead in search of fish. The steep and rocky east side of Rattlesnake Hill is frequented by turkey vultures, porcupines, and bobcats.

Directions: *From Route 2, take Route 202 south for 2 miles to the parking area and Gate 29 on the left. From Route 9, follow Route 202 north for approximately 18 miles to Gate 29 on the right.*

Ownership: MDC (413) 323-7221

Size: 1,500 acres   **Closest Town:** Orange

Fresh drillings and wood chips are a sure sign that a pileated woodpecker has been at work on this white pine. The large cavities are made as these birds search for carpenter ants.
BILL BYRNE

42

Description: Stone foundations, old roadways, and ornamental trees testify that Dana Common was once the center of the town of Dana. Most other traces of human settlement have been reclaimed by nature since the creation of Quabbin Reservoir in the 1930s. Fields and openings throughout this site are maintained for watershed management and wildlife habitat diversity. The mixed deciduous and coniferous forest is bordered by Pottapaug Pond and interspersed with beaver swamps, hillside seeps, ledge outcrops, red pine plantations, and a sedge meadow. The Gate 40 road ends at the shoreline of the reservoir at a site known as Graves Landing, providing viewing access to a large, shallow section of the reservoir.

Viewing Information: From Gate 40, the paved roadway winds 1.8 miles toward Dana Common. Pottapaug Pond will be visible on the left. Watch Pottapaug for swimming beavers, particularly early and late in the day, and listen for the chattering of the kingfisher. The uniform rows of red pine, planted originally to hold soils, are now being thinned and harvested for pulp wood. Brown creepers and red squirrels favor the pines. Stone walls and foundations at Dana Common are shelter for black racers and ribbon snakes. Shed snake skins can be found around the stonework. Continue another 2.2 miles through woodlands inhabited by barred owls, chestnut-sided warblers, dark-eyed juncos, and eastern coyotes. At Graves Landing, glass the shoreline and island trees for perched bald eagles. Scan the surface waters for common loons and mergansers and peer into the clear shallows where rock bass and smallmouth bass cruise over the gravel bottom. During drought periods, the reservoir level can drop dramatically, creating exposed mud flats. These flats can be an excellent place to see migrating shorebirds like greater yellowlegs and semipalmated sandpipers in the fall.

Directions: *From Route 122 in Petersham, follow Route 32A south for 3 miles to the gravel parking area and Gate 40 on the right. From the center of Hardwick, follow Route 32A north for approximately 6.5 miles to the parking area and Gate 40 on the left.*

Ownership: MDC (413) 323-7221

Size: 1,100 acres   **Closest Town:** Petersham

VALLEY

Even though Massachusetts has a human population of more than 6 million, many wildlife species have naturally expanded their range and now call the Bay State home. A few interesting examples are: moose, coyotes, fishers, and ravens.

Description: Quabbin Park combines panoramic views, trails, a paved roadway, and a visitor center. Located at the southern end of Quabbin Reservoir, the park links Winsor Dam and Goodnough Dike, the structures that contain Quabbin's waters. Enfield Lookout provides a magnificent four-season view of the reservoir. Also within the park are an observation tower, orchard, wetlands, the Swift River, and various stages of successional forest.

Viewing Information: Stop at the visitor center, located just west of Winsor Dam, for maps and information. The view north often includes common loons, Canada geese, and other water birds. Cross the dam and turn right just before the spillway bridge and drive to the outflow of the Swift River. Scan the clear waters for the shadow of a rainbow trout. Check the spillway for common ravens and eastern phoebes, then continue up the roadway along the southwest side of Quabbin Hill to the rotary near the top. The top of the hill offers hawk-watching opportunities and the Quabbin observation tower. A hike from the rotary to the nearby apple orchard may reveal white-tailed deer, gray foxes, and colorful redstarts. The road continues to Enfield Lookout, the premier winter bald eagle viewing site in the state, but don't overlook the chance to see eagles, eastern coyotes, and wild turkeys at other times of the year.

Directions: From the intersection of routes 9 and 202 in Belchertown, take Route 9 east 3.3 miles to the Quabbin Reservoir/Winsor Dam entrance on the left. From routes 9 and 32 in Ware, follow Route 9 west for about 6 miles to the Quabbin Reservoir sign and entrance on right.

Ownership: MDC (413) 323-7221

Size: 3,100 acres   **Closest Town:** Belchertown

An adult bald eagle comes in for a landing on icy Quabbin Reservoir. In late February, eagle numbers peak; more than 50 eagles may be present, searching for fish, waterfowl, and carrion. BILL BYRNE

18. HERMAN COVEY WILDLIFE MANAGEMENT AREA AND MCLAUGHLIN TROUT HATCHERY

Description: The Quabbin Reservoir feeds cold, clear water through Winsor Dam, thereby forming the Swift River. Once south of Route 9, much of the river is part of the Covey Wildlife Management Area. In addition to the river frontage, the area is made up of beaver ponds, mixed hardwood forests, and open meadows. The McLaughlin Hatchery is the largest trout rearing facility in the state.

Viewing Information: Make a quick stop at the McLaughlin Trout Hatchery (open 365 days a year from 8 A.M. to 4 P.M.) to view and feed the six- to ten-pound rainbow trout in the display pool. Hatchery tours are available to larger groups by reservation. The management area parking lot is opposite DFW's Connecticut Valley District office. Visit the office during business hours for maps and current wildlife information. A hike on the property during summer months often reveals beavers, great blue herons, red-eyed vireos, and great-crested flycatchers. Look for castings of undigested fur and bone left by barred owls under the dead lower branches of white pine trees. White-tailed deer feed in the meadows in spring and regularly travel to stands of red oak in the fall in search of acorns.

Directions: *From the intersection of routes 9 and 202 in Belchertown, take Route 9 east for about 4 miles to a right turn on East Street. Follow East Street for 1 mile to McLaughlin Hatchery. Continue another mile to the district office and management area parking lot.*

Ownership: DFW (413) 323-7632; McLaughlin Trout Hatchery (413) 323-7671

Size: 1,400 acres   **Closest Town:** Belchertown

The big ones that didn't get away are on display at the McLaughlin Trout Hatchery. About 500,000 pounds of brook, brown, and rainbow trout are produced annually in DFW hatcheries.
BILL BYRNE

VALLEY

45

19. ARCADIA WILDLIFE SANCTUARY

Description: The sanctuary features meadows, deciduous and coniferous forests, and an oxbow lake. The Connecticut River Valley is a natural migration flyway for songbirds and waterfowl.

Viewing Information: The visitor center has details on recent wildlife observations and may be able to suggest a current viewing opportunity. The viewing tower can be a particularly good vantage point when looking for mallards, wood ducks, great blue and green herons, kingfishers, and forest songbirds. A variety of educational and interpretive programs are held year-round. Staff naturalists add insight and help wildlife watchers understand the features of a wetland, woodland, or field habitat. The sanctuary is closed Mondays.

Directions: *From Interstate 91, take exit 18 and follow Route 5 south. After 1.5 miles turn right on East Street and follow it for about 1 mile to Fort Hill Road. Turn right on Fort Hill Road and follow sanctuary signs to the entrance.*

Ownership: MAS (413) 584-3009

Size: 597 acres   **Closest Town:** Easthampton

20. SKINNER STATE PARK

Description: Striking views of the Connecticut River, Connecticut Valley, and Holyoke Range await visitors to the Summit House, perched atop Mount Holyoke. Running east/west, the Holyoke Range is breached by the Connecticut River, forming a steep-sided pass guarded by Mount Holyoke to the east and mounts Nonotuck and Tom to the west. The valley and range are natural flyways for migrating birds.

Viewing Information: From the entrance gate, hike the steep trail to the Summit House. Chipmunks and gray squirrels are common. Black-furred or melanistic gray squirrels can also be seen. Listen for the hoarse croaking of common ravens cruising above the ledge slopes. When the entrance gate is open, drive to the Summit House and watch for turkey vultures, red-tailed hawks, and American kestrels from the porch. During spring and fall migrations, ospreys and broad-winged and sharp-shinned hawks make regular appearances. Watch for bald eagles over the river and, in fall, listen for the faint honking calls of Canada and snow geese flying south. The 2,900-acre Holyoke Range State Park is located just to the east.

Directions: *From the Massachusetts Turnpike (Interstate 90), take I-91 north to Route 9. Follow Route 9 east to Route 47 south. Stay on Route 47 for approximately 4 miles to the park entrance on the left.*

Ownership: DEM (413) 586-0350

Size: 390 acres   **Closest Town:** Hadley

21. MOUNT TOM STATE RESERVATION

Description: The Mount Tom Range is an extension of the Holyoke Range to the east, cut off by the waters of the Connecticut River. Mount Tom and her sister peaks contribute to the valley flyway by creating thermal air currents and updrafts that aid migrating songbirds and raptors. Scenic views and fall foliage are bonuses at this site.

Viewing Information: Songbirds in the spring and hawks in the fall aptly describes the primary attractions at Mount Tom. Look and listen for blackburnian warblers, veeries, and ovenbirds in the mixed forests, and pause at Lake Bray to look for green herons fishing the shallows or eastern kingbirds chasing insects from the treetops. At the upper elevations scenic views and hawk-watching overlooks are accessible by car. A short hike to the Goat Peak tower puts you at the top of the ridge, where views looking down on broad-winged and sharp-shinned hawks are possible. Organized hawk counts are conducted during fall months.

Directions: *From the Massachusetts Turnpike (Interstate 90), take I-91 north to exit 17A for Route 5. Take Route 5 north for 4 miles to Reservation Road and the entrance on the left.*

Ownership: DEM (413) 527-4805

Size: 1,850 acres   **Closest Town:** Easthampton

VALLEY

A red-tailed hawk scans its surroundings for a mouse, vole, or rabbit. Its feathers are puffed out to trap air and retain body heat. Red-tails are conspicuous along major highways as they hunt the grassy margins and medians. BILL BYRNE

22. BARRETT FISHWAY

Description: The Robert E. Barrett Fishway at Holyoke Dam is an urban viewing site offering a seasonal opportunity to witness the spawning migration of an estimated 1 million fish in the Connecticut River. Operated as part of the Hadley Falls hydroelectric generating station, the fishway is designed to lift fish over the otherwise impassable dam.

Viewing Information: The exhibit area offers information on the migrating fish. Pass through the hydroelectric plant to the observation deck for a view of the dam and river. Look for fish splashing at the base of the falls and for opportunistic herring gulls and double-crested cormorants trying to catch a meal. In the viewing room, three windows flank the 300-foot fish passage flume and interpreters are on duty to share their knowledge. After each lift, American shad, blueback herring, sea lampreys, American eels, and Atlantic salmon make their way past the viewing windows toward spawning streams upriver. Salmon are sometimes taken from the flume for transport to nearby fish hatcheries as part of a multistate salmon restoration project. Watch for resident warm-water fish such as pumpkinseeds, largemouth bass, and catfish. A typical visit will take 30 to 40 minutes. The fishway operates only during the short spawning run, which is typically from early May to mid-June and is dependent on weather and water conditions. It is open Wednesday through Sunday from 9 A.M. to 5 P.M. Call for updated information.

Directions: *From Interstate 91 south, take exit 17A. Turn left at the foot of the ramp onto Route 141 east. Bear right at the second set of traffic lights and follow for six more sets of lights to a left turn on Route 116, Main Street. Take Route 116 north for 1 mile to the fishway entrance on the left just BEFORE South Hadley Falls bridge. From I-91 north, take I-391 to Holyoke/Main Street exit. Turn right at the foot of the ramp onto Route 116. Proceed on Route 116 north to the fishway entrance as above.*

Ownership: NU (413) 659-3714

Size: 1 acre   **Closest City:** Holyoke

Conservation projects have resulted in the restoration of bald eagles, peregrine falcons, wild turkeys, and Atlantic salmon to the wild in Massachusetts.

Description: Oak and hickory forests command the uplands, giving way to a scenic brook and river below. Habitat in the riparian corridor, the area along the waterways, provides cover and travel lanes for a variety of animals. The sanctuary is a licensed wildlife rehabilitation facility and houses native species that cannot be returned to the wild. Exhibits display these long-term "patients," giving wildlife viewers unique, close-up looks at otherwise elusive creatures.

Viewing Information: Scarlet tanagers, red-eyed vireos, and ovenbirds are regular nesting birds in the hardwood forests. Yellow warblers are found nearer the waterways. A variety of butterflies use open areas and are conspicuous in spring and summer. A viewing platform and boardwalk provide enhanced access while protecting fragile habitat. Staff naturalists provide information at the visitor center and conduct regular tours of the grounds. The sanctuary is closed Mondays.

Directions: *From Interstate 91, take exit 2 for Route 83. Follow signs for Route 83 toward East Longmeadow. Stay on Route 83 through East Longmeadow. About 1.5 miles beyond the center of town, turn left on Hampden Road and follow it to its end. Turn right on Somers Road, proceed 0.25 mile, turn left on Main Street, and follow it for 2 miles to the center of Hampden. Continue straight for 0.5 mile to the site entrance on the left.*

Ownership: MAS (413) 566-8034

Size: 356 acres   **Closest Town:** Hampden

VALLEY

A garden spider has trapped a honey bee in its web. The web reflects the morning dew as the spider subdues its prey.
BILL BYRNE

49

CENTRAL REGION—WOODLANDS AND WETLANDS

Central Massachusetts is characterized by rolling hills, mixed woodlands, and meandering rivers including the Nashua, Assabet, and Blackstone. Many brooks and streams have been impounded by beavers, giving rise to new wild-life-rich wetlands. Numerous lakes and ponds dot the landscape where mixed forests of oak, hickory, pine, and hemlock are dominant. Wachusett Mountain rises above the surrounding hills, providing one of the most scenic views in the region. There are 12 wildlife viewing sites featuring a variety of opportunities to see hawks, bats, and bluebirds, or to paddle a canoe trail.

A waterfall in this Massachusetts forest provides habitat for aquatic plants, amphibians, and fish. Massachusetts has a wealth of waterways and wetlands which are recharged by an average annual rainfall of 45 inches. BILL BYRNE

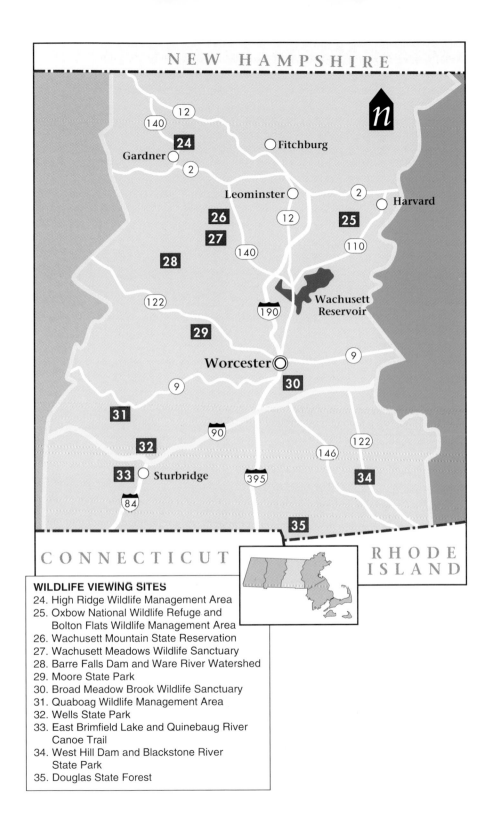

NEW HAMPSHIRE

12
140
24
Gardner○
Fitchburg○
2

Leominster○
2
Harvard○
26
12
25
27
110
28
140

122
Wachusett Reservoir
190
29
9
Worcester◉
9
30
31
90
32
122
146
33 ○ Sturbridge
395
34
84
35

CONNECTICUT
RHODE ISLAND

WILDLIFE VIEWING SITES
24. High Ridge Wildlife Management Area
25. Oxbow National Wildlife Refuge and
    Bolton Flats Wildlife Management Area
26. Wachusett Mountain State Reservation
27. Wachusett Meadows Wildlife Sanctuary
28. Barre Falls Dam and Ware River Watershed
29. Moore State Park
30. Broad Meadow Brook Wildlife Sanctuary
31. Quaboag Wildlife Management Area
32. Wells State Park
33. East Brimfield Lake and Quinebaug River
    Canoe Trail
34. West Hill Dam and Blackstone River
    State Park
35. Douglas State Forest

24. HIGH RIDGE WILDLIFE MANAGEMENT AREA

Description: Open grasslands and their associated bird community are a featured attraction at this site. Mixed hardwood and white pine stands are interspersed with fields and wetlands. A Department of Corrections facility abuts the property and is off-limits to the public.

Viewing Information: More than 100 bluebird nest boxes dot the abandoned roadsides and field edges, offering a unique opportunity to observe cavity-nesting birds. Virtually every box is occupied during the nesting season with tree swallows, bluebirds, house wrens, or black-capped chickadees. Watch the nest boxes from a short distance away and wait for an adult bird to bring food for the youngsters inside. Food deliveries are frequent when there are multiple mouths to feed. The grassy fields are also used by bobolinks. American kestrels hunt over the open spaces, nesting under the eaves of abandoned buildings. Check soft soil for red fox tracks.

Directions: *From Route 2, take Route 140 north for 2 miles to the Smith Street parking area on the right.*

Ownership: DFW (508) 835-3607

Size: 2,018 acres   **Closest City:** Gardner

25. OXBOW NATIONAL WILDLIFE REFUGE AND BOLTON FLATS WILDLIFE MANAGEMENT AREA

Description: The Nashua and Still rivers wind their way through floodplain hardwoods and along wet meadows and open agricultural fields. Changes in the river courses are marked by small, isolated oxbow ponds. Springtime flooding creates prime conditions for waterfowl and amphibians.

Viewing Information: The floodplain associated with these two areas is a premier central Massachusetts birding location during periods of springtime high water. Scores of mallards, teal, and wood ducks are drawn to inundated fields and forests. As the waters recede, look and listen for woodcock courtship flights over open areas at dusk. Vernal pools dot the sites and serve as breeding habitat for spring peepers, wood frogs, and spotted salamanders. Rare Blanding's turtles are found in slower sections of the rivers.

Directions: *From Route 2, follow Route 110 south to Harvard and continue for 2 miles. Turn right on Still River Depot Road and follow it across the railroad tracks to the Oxbow entrance. For Bolton Flats, continue south on Route 110 to the entrance at a large red barn on the right.*

Ownership: Oxbow NWR, USFWS (508) 443-4661; Bolton Flats WMA, DFW (508) 835-3607

Size: 2,523 acres   **Closest Town:** Harvard

26. WACHUSETT MOUNTAIN STATE RESERVATION

Description: At 2,006 feet, Wachusett Mountain rises above the surrounding central Massachusetts countryside, providing a beautiful view in all directions. One of the premier hawk-watching sites in the state, the summit of Wachusett Mountain is a rocky ridgetop bald, giving the site a subalpine appeal.

Viewing Information: From the visitor center, hike or drive toward the summit, watching and listening for yellow-bellied sapsuckers, chestnut-sided warblers, and cedar waxwings. Porcupine trails weave along the rocky slopes. Red-tailed hawks and turkey vultures may be seen soaring over the flanks of the mountain at many times of year, but September and October are the prime hawk-watching months. The summit and two other viewing lookouts below provide the best vantage for seeing numbers of broad-winged, red-shouldered, and sharp-shinned hawks as well as passing ospreys and bald eagles. Organized hawk counts are popular at the summit from early September to late October. A downhill ski area limits access and viewing opportunities from December through March.

Directions: *From Route 2, follow Route 140 south for 3.7 miles to Mile Hill Road on the right. Follow Mile Hill Road past the ski area to the reservation and visitor center on the right. From Interstate 190, take Route 140 north for 6.1 miles to Mile Hill Road on the left.*

Ownership: DEM (508) 464-2987

Size: 2,850 acres   **Closest Town:** Princeton

CENTRAL

Hawk-watchers line up at the summit of Wachusett Mountain for the annual fall spectacle of thousands of hawks on the wing. For information on hawks and hawk-watching contact: Eastern Mass. Hawk Watch, 254 Arlington St., Medford, MA 02155. BILL BYRNE

Description: Forested wetlands, grassy fields bounded by stone walls, small ponds, and a well-defined trail system characterize this site. Situated in the shadow of Wachusett Mountain, Wachusett Meadows is the focus of an ongoing breeding bird survey conducted annually since 1964. Data gathered here shed light on long-term trends in populations of birds collectively known as "neotropical migrants," a term used to classify species dependent on the northern forests for breeding and the tropics for wintering.

Viewing Information: Barn swallows flash across the driveway, flying to and from their nests during breeding season. Warblers, colorful members of the neotropical migrant group, are found throughout the forests; ovenbirds, common yellowthroats, and chestnut-sided warblers are the most abundant. Seventeen species of warblers have been recorded as breeding here. The fields are used by bobolinks and the stone walls function as both home and highway for chipmunks. At 1,300 feet, Brown Hill is an ideal spot to witness the autumn hawk migration and the dazzling foliage. As fall fades into winter the site can be used to sharpen tracking skills. Look for the distinctive signs of minks and fishers in fresh snow and envision these weasels actively searching the walls, wetlands, and forests for prey. Staff is available to answer questions and interpretive walks are scheduled regularly. The sanctuary is closed Mondays.

Directions: *From Route 140, take Route 62 west to Princeton. Continue on Route 62 for 0.7 mile beyond the center of town to Goodnow Road on the right. The site is 1 mile ahead on Goodnow Road.*

Ownership: MAS (508) 464-2712

Size: 1,008 acres   **Closest Town:** Princeton

A fisher, a large member of the weasel family, is secretive by nature and seldom seen. Its tracks betray its presence and often lead to stone walls, dead trees, and thickets where prey species like squirrels and chipmunks are found. BILL BYRNE

Description: Extensive wetlands border pine and oak forests, fields, and the Ware River itself, creating habitat edges attractive to a variety of wildlife.

Viewing Information: Accessible by car, canoe, or on foot, this extensive area takes time to explore. From the dam, bluebirds and ravens are frequently seen. A carry-down canoe launch site is located near the dam. On the river, rough-winged swallows and belted kingfishers fly low over the water and yellow and pine warblers can be heard along the forested banks. When road conditions permit, the interior of the site is accessible by vehicle. Eastern meadowlarks, alder flycatchers, wild turkeys, and white-tailed deer can be seen in and around open fields.

Directions: *From Route 2 in Gardner, take Route 68 south to Hubbardston. Turn right on Elm Street, which becomes Barre Road, and follow it for 2.5 miles to the intersection with Route 62. Proceed straight across Route 62 to the entrance to Barre Falls Dam.*

Ownership: Barre Falls Dam, USACE (508) 928-4712; Ware River Watershed, MDC (413) 323-7221

Size: 22,000 acres   **Closest Town:** Hubbardston

The wild turkey was restored to the fields and forests of Massachusetts in the 1970s after an absence of more than 100 years. Watch for the courtship display of "toms" in spring and large flocks of hens and "jakes" near dairy farms in winter.
BILL BYRNE

CENTRAL

55

29. MOORE STATE PARK

Description: Moore State Park combines scenic and historic qualities with one of the most interesting seasonal wildlife viewing opportunities in the state. The lush and extensive laurels and rhododendrons remind the visitor that the park was once a well-manicured estate, while the rushing waters of Turkey Hill Brook harken back to the 1700s, a time when running water meant power to run grist and sawmills. Nature has reclaimed much of the land, and wildlife now dominates what was once a thriving village.

Viewing Information: A colony of little brown bats spends the late spring and summer roosting in a specially constructed bat house. Just to the northwest of the spillway, which channels water from Eames Pond into Turkey Hill Brook, the bat house has a single opening through which the bats pass on their nightly feeding forays. Watch the opening from a distance so the bats are not disturbed. Once bats are seen emerging, usually just before dusk, move to the pond shoreline to take advantage of the available light and look for bats silhouetted against the sky. During daylight hours walk the Eames Pond trail and watch for Canada geese, wood ducks, great blue herons, tree swallows, eastern kingbirds, painted turtles, beavers, and muskrats. In winter, cross-country skiing along the edges of fields and meadows reveals tracks of white-tailed deer, red foxes, and eastern coyotes.

Directions: *From Worcester, take Route 122 north to Paxton. Turn left on Route 31. The park entrance is 1 mile on the right.*

Ownership: DEM (508) 792-3969

Size: 600 acres   **Closest Town:** Paxton

Turkey Hill Brook rushes past the sawmill at Moore State Park. Roaring spring meltwater, summer floral blooms, and fall foliage enhance wildlife viewing.
BILL BYRNE

30. BROAD MEADOW BROOK WILDLIFE SANCTUARY

Description: Located in Massachusetts' second largest city, Broad Meadow Brook preserves open space and provides outdoor environmental education in an otherwise highly developed light-industrial area. Second-growth woodlands are reclaiming formerly cleared or burned sections of the property as nature slowly obscures the past influences of humans.

Viewing Information: Raccoons, opossums, striped skunks, cottontail rabbits, and red-tailed hawks are regularly seen. Migratory songbirds stop to rest and feed in the springtime as they travel toward larger, unbroken forested tracts to the north. Wetlands harbor amphibians and reptiles including red-backed salamanders, garter snakes, and snapping turtles. A surprising variety of butterflies has been documented at this urban site. Programs are presented by staff throughout the year with an emphasis on suburban habitat and wildlife conservation. The sanctuary is closed Mondays.

Directions: *From the Massachusetts Turnpike (Interstate 90), take exit 11 for Route 122. Turn left at the traffic light at the end of the ramp onto Route 122 north. Follow Route 122 for about 1 mile to Route 20, turn left, and follow Route 20 to the first traffic light. Turn right onto Massasoit Road and follow it for 0.5 mile to the site entrance on the left.*

Ownership: MAS (508) 753-6087

Size: 267 acres   **Closest City:** Worcester

CENTRAL

Backyards and backwoods are home to the common garter snake. Any area providing frogs, insects, water, and cover is potential garter snake habitat. BILL BYRNE

57

31. QUABOAG WILDLIFE MANAGEMENT AREA

Description: The waters of the Quaboag River spread out into extensive areas of cattail marsh and shrub swamp before the land rises to brushy fields and stands of red oak, maple, and shagbark hickory.

Viewing Information: The Quaboag River is best experienced by canoe, allowing the wildlife watcher to drift with the flow and become part of the wetlands. Ring-necked ducks are regular spring migrants along with common mergansers. Large numbers of ducks gather to the east at nearby Quaboag Pond. The marsh is nesting habitat for rare American bitterns. Listen for their distinctive throaty "oonk-a-lunk" call from the cattails. The waters support a healthy population of northern pike, which spawn in the vegetated shallows just after ice-out. Wild turkeys and woodcock can be found around the upland fields.

Directions: *From Route 9 in Brookfield, take Route 148 south to the bridge over the Quaboag River. Canoes can be launched near the bridge. Continue south on Route 148 to a right turn onto Long Hill Road. Follow Long Hill Road to parking areas on the right.*

Ownership: DFW (508) 835-3607

Size: 1,107 acres   **Closest Town:** East Brookfield

A fish splashes at the feet of a great blue heron as the stately bird wades through the shallows. Great blues are found statewide during warmer months, retreating to the coast and points south for the winter.
BILL BYRNE

32. WELLS STATE PARK

Description: Mixed oak uplands are interrupted by active and abandoned beaver flowages and their associated wooded swamps. A power line right-of-way, Walker Pond, and the narrow Carpenter Rocks ridge add further diversity to the property.

Viewing Information: The grassy margin of the entrance road is a good place to spot woodchucks and cottontail rabbits. A beaver impoundment is located on the right just before the main parking area. Northern water snakes and painted turtles often sun themselves on the beaver dam. Take the Mill Pond Trail or a steeper climb to Carpenter Rocks and look for downy woodpeckers and hermit thrushes along the way. Turkey vultures can be seen gliding over the ridge. A stop at the edge of Walker Pond may reveal a chain pickerel hovering motionless among the aquatic vegetation. At night, listen for barred, great horned, and saw-whet owls and the high-pitched squeaks of northern flying squirrels. Spring peepers and American toads add music and life to the springtime darkness. Wells State Park offers 60 campsites, ideal for wildlife watchers interested in an overnight outdoor experience. Maps and other park information are available at the park office. Guided interpretive programs are conducted during summer months.

Directions: From the Massachusetts Turnpike (Interstate 90), take exit 9 and proceed east on Route 20 for 2 miles to its junction with Route 49. Turn left on Route 49 and follow it for 1 mile to the park entrance on the left.

Ownership: DEM (508) 347-9257

Size: 1,500 acres   **Closest Town:** Sturbridge

CENTRAL

Look for ruffed grouse in abandoned apple orchards, overgrown pastures, and mixed woodlands. Grouse can also be seen feeding on the buds of aspen trees in early spring.
BILL BYRNE

33. EAST BRIMFIELD LAKE AND QUINEBAUG RIVER CANOE TRAIL

Description: A 7-mile canoe trail winds its way through broad wetlands and along forested banks before emptying into East Brimfield Lake.

Viewing Information: Flat water and no portages allow the canoeist to concentrate on looking ahead as the Quinebaug River meanders slowly around tight bends thick with shrubby vegetation. Red-winged blackbirds are constant companions and beaver sign is evident. Green and great blue herons, minks, and otters feed along the riverbanks on fish and frogs.

Directions: *From the Massachusetts Turnpike (Interstate 90), take exit 9 for Interstate 84 and take the first exit (3B). Follow Route 20 west for 4 miles to Holland-East Brimfield Road on the left. Follow Holland-East Brimfield Road for 3 miles to Morse Road on the right. Follow canoe signs to the launch area.*

Ownership: USACE (508) 347-3705

Size: 7-mile canoe trail   **Closest Town:** Sturbridge

34. WEST HILL DAM AND BLACKSTONE RIVER STATE PARK

Description: These sites present a variety of viewing opportunities in the Blackstone River Valley, long regarded as a cornerstone of the American Industrial Revolution. The Blackstone and West rivers and the historic Blackstone Canal provide vital riparian corridors linking areas of wildlife habitat.

Viewing Information: Maps and information are available at the West Hill Dam Ranger Station and Blackstone River State Park Visitor Center. The bridge over the dam's spillway is a nesting site for northern rough-winged swallows. Black racers inhabit stone walls and old foundations. Trails beginning at the Riverbend Farm Visitor Center at the park follow the canal and river, where painted turtles and muskrats are regularly seen. Rails inhabit the river's backwater at Rice City Pond. Lookout Rock offers a scenic overlook of the valley.

Directions: *From the Massachusetts Turnpike (Interstate 90), take Route 122 south to Uxbridge. Turn left at the traffic light on Hartford Avenue and follow it for 1 mile to Oak Street on the right. Riverbend Visitor Center is just down Oak Street on the left. West Hill Dam Ranger Station is off Hartford Avenue, 0.75 mile beyond the Oak Street turnoff. Follow the West Hill Dam signs to the entrance.*

Ownership: West Hill Dam, USACE (508) 278-2511; Blackstone River State Park, DEM (508) 278-6486

Size: 1,562 acres   **Closest Town:** Uxbridge

35. DOUGLAS STATE FOREST

Description: A mix of woods and waters aptly describes Douglas State Forest. Wallum Lake borders the property. Wetlands, vernal pools, and a cedar swamp dot the diverse hardwood, white pine, and hemlock stands of the interior.

Viewing Information: The winding trails are good places to watch for American toads and the orange land-dwelling young of the red-spotted newt. From the interpretive center, follow the Cedar Swamp Trail and turn left onto the Bird Blind Trail to visit the viewing platform and observation blind. Sit quietly to encounter a variety of songbirds. Chickadees, nuthatches, blue jays, eastern towhees, and tufted titmice are regular visitors. Continue on the Cedar Swamp Trail through an historic quarry and on to the boardwalk. During all seasons, look for sign of resident mammals like red foxes, gray and red squirrels, chipmunks, and deer mice.

Directions: *From the Massachusetts Turnpike (Interstate 90), take I-395 south to exit 2, Route 16 east. Follow Route 16 for 5 miles to Cedar Street on the right. Take Cedar Street through the intersection and onto Wallum Pond Road, and continue to the entrance on the right.*

Ownership: DEM (508) 476-7872

Size: 4,600 acres   **Closest Town:** Douglas

The red eft is the juvenile stage of the red-spotted newt. After spending 2 to 3 years in this terrestrial stage the eft returns to the water to breed as an aquatic adult. Efts are found in moist woodlands while the adults prefer clear lakes and slow-moving streams.
BILL BYRNE

NORTHEAST REGION—MERRIMACK VALLEY, NORTH SHORE, AND GREATER BOSTON

The waters of the Merrimack, Concord, and Charles rivers find their way to the ocean in this densely populated area of the Bay State. The mixing of fresh and salt water at the mouth of the Merrimack River provides particularly rich wildlife habitat for resident and migratory wildlife alike. The exposed, rocky headlands of Cape Ann jut into the Atlantic while the more sheltered Harbor Islands lie in the shadow of the Boston skyline. Inland, freshwater wetlands are attractive to waterfowl and wading birds. This region features 16 wildlife viewing sites, providing access to surf, salt marshes, and sanctuaries.

Plum Island is part of the Parker River National Wildlife Refuge (Site 38). The transitions between beach, dune, upland, and salt marsh are evident in this aerial view of the refuge's barrier beach ecosystem. BILL BYRNE

WILDLIFE VIEWING SITES
36. Salisbury Beach State Reservation
37. Maudslay State Park
38. Parker River National Wildlife Refuge
39. Halibut Point
40. Richard T. Crane, Jr. Memorial Reservation
41. Ipswich River Wildlife Sanctuary
42. Delaney Wildlife Management Area
43. Great Meadows National Wildlife Refuge
44. Drumlin Farm Wildlife Sanctuary
45. Belle Isle Marsh Reservation
46. Boston Harbor Islands State Park
47. World's End Reservation
48. Broadmoor Wildlife Sanctuary
49. Blue Hills Reservation and
     Trailside Museum
50. Moose Hill Wildlife Sanctuary
51. Bristol-Blake State Reservation and Stony
     Brook Wildlife Sanctuary

Description: The Merrimack River meets the Atlantic Ocean at Salisbury Beach, creating a rich and dynamic environment for migrating shorebirds, waterfowl, and wintering harbor seals.

Viewing Information: Spring, fall, and winter are the featured wildlife viewing seasons at Salisbury Beach. Extensive brackish wetlands are visible from the entrance roadway. These wetlands attract migrating black ducks, green-winged teal, and great blue herons. From the boardwalk and viewing platforms, watch the tidal zone along the beach for pectoral, solitary, and least sandpipers as they search for invertebrates in the wet sand. White-winged and surf scoters can be seen flying low over open water or bobbing in loose flocks among the offshore waves. In winter and spring the waters bordering the campground offer prime viewing for harbor seals. These large marine mammals frequently "haul out" on sandbars, rocks, and jetties to rest and bask.

Directions: *From Interstate 95, take Route 110 east to Route 1A in Salisbury. Follow Route 1A north for 2 miles to the entrance on the right.*

Ownership: DEM (508) 462-4481

Size: 521 acres   **Closest Town:** Salisbury

Harbor seals bask at low tide to rest and groom. When wet, the seals' fur appears shiny and black, then changes to a softer, pearl-gray color as it dries. BILL BYRNE

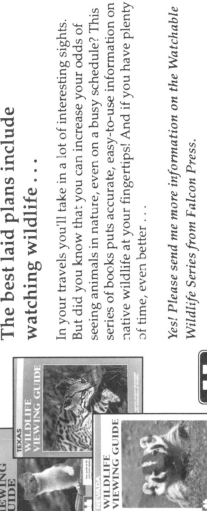

Description: This former private estate encompasses forest, fields, maintained landscapes, and almost 2 miles of frontage along the Merrimack River. Mature white pine groves shadow a dense mountain laurel understory which contrasts with nearby mixed hardwood stands. Wetlands, ponds, and a vernal pool complete the habitat picture.

Viewing Information: The visitor center can provide a feel for both the human and natural history of the site. A wildlife list, plant list, and maps are available describing the fauna and flora and the more than 16 miles of trails and overlooks. Enjoy the grounds and gardens of the estate, where gray squirrels, eastern chipmunks, red foxes, and ruby-throated hummingbirds can be found among the rhododendrons, dogwoods, and azaleas. Muskrats, river otters, green frogs, and painted turtles use the ponds and wetlands. Great horned owls, brown creepers, tufted titmice, and white-tailed deer inhabit the woodlands. In winter, bald eagles use the open waters of the Merrimack River in their search for fish and waterfowl. An area along the river is closed in the winter to protect roosting eagles, but eagles may be seen from Deer Island and the Chain Bridge, just downriver from the park.

Directions: *From Interstate 95, take Route 113 east to Noble Street. Turn left, continue to a stop sign, and turn left on Ferry Road. Bear left at the fork, following signs to the park entrance. From Interstate 495, take Route 110 east to the second set of lights and turn right on Merrill Street. Cross the Merrimack River via the Chain Bridge and Deer Island. Continue straight at the intersection where Merrill Street becomes Spofford Street. Turn right onto Ferry Road just BEFORE the stop sign at the top of the hill. Follow signs to the park entrance.*

Ownership: DEM (508) 465-7223

Size: 480 acres   **Closest Town:** Newburyport

The river otter is a highly social, often vocal, aquatic member of the weasel family. Otters create furrowed slides down steep stream banks on snow or mud or alternately run and slide on their bellies across pond ice.
BILL BYRNE

38. PARKER RIVER NATIONAL WILDLIFE REFUGE

Description: Parker River National Wildlife Refuge's natural barrier beach dune complex and sheltered salt marsh represent one of the few examples of this habitat in New England. Dune grass, false heather, beach plum, willows, and pines are predominant in the uplands, while the salt marsh and 262 acres of impounded freshwater wetlands attract hundreds of species of birds.

Viewing Information: Migratory waterfowl by the thousands descend on Parker River annually, with peak concentrations reaching 25,000 during late fall and early winter. Black ducks, green-winged teal, pintails, gadwalls, and buffleheads are seasonal visitors. Shorebirds such as dowitchers, willets, glossy ibises, and greater yellowlegs take advantage of shallow, nutrient-rich "pannes" to feed on invertebrates. In colder months, rough-legged hawks can be seen hunting for small mammals. Snowy owls occasionally winter on the refuge. Harbor seals winter in the ocean waters surrounding the refuge and can be seen as they bob beyond the surf or haul out on the beaches or at Emerson's Rocks. Observation towers, blinds, trails, and a 6.4-mile roadway between the salt marsh and dunes provide views and excellent access.

Directions: From Interstate 95, take exit 57 for Route 113, Newburyport. Follow Route 113 east, which becomes High Street, for approximately 5 miles to a traffic light at its intersection with Rolfe's Lane. Turn left and continue to a stop sign at the junction with the Plum Island Turnpike. Turn right, cross the bridge over the Parker River, then turn right at the first intersection, to the refuge entrance.

Ownership: USFWS (508) 465-5753

Size: 4,662 acres   **Closest Town:** Newburyport

Parker River National Wildlife Refuge is a mecca for both birds and bird-watchers. Yellowlegs and sandpipers are drawn to the area by the expansive habitat.
BILL BYRNE

66

39. HALIBUT POINT

Description: A granite headland rises 50 feet above the ocean, creating tidal pools and spectacular surf during northeast storms. Bayberry, greenbrier, and shadbush cling to the poor soil, and scrub oaks show the influence of strong winds and past fires.

Viewing Information: Halibut Point offers a commanding view of Ipswich Bay and the New Hampshire coastline. Goldeneyes, scoters, and scaups can be seen offshore. Black ducks linger near rocks and pools. Seabirds can be viewed in winter months, and coastal storms sometimes drive species such as gannets, guillemots, and jaegers close to the rocky coast. In tidal areas around the bluff, snails, rock crabs, and periwinkles can be found in pools left by the falling tide. *USE CAUTION WHEN TRAVERSING SLIPPERY ROCKS.*

Directions: *From Route 128, take Route 127 (Eastern Avenue) north toward Rockport for 3 miles. Stay on Route 127 as it turns left and becomes Railroad Avenue. Continue 2.4 miles to Gott Avenue on the right. Halibut Point parking area is on the right as you proceed on Gott Avenue.*

Ownership: DEM (508) 546-2997; TTOR (508) 356-4351

Size: 68 acres   **Closest Town:** Rockport

40. RICHARD T. CRANE, JR. MEMORIAL RESERVATION

Description: A 4-mile-long barrier beach with associated dunes, marsh, and maritime forest protects Essex Bay and the Essex and Ipswich river estuaries from the storm-tossed Atlantic Ocean. The 59-room Great House, the center of the former estate, is set on Castle Hill overlooking landscaped grounds, remnant formal gardens, and the beach beyond.

Viewing Information: A 1-mile interpretive trail explains the barrier beach system and leads to a bordering wooded area where dunes are encroaching and claiming the trees in a graphic demonstration of beach processes. Terns and piping plovers nest on exposed beaches while herons and egrets hunt the protected marshes. Waterfowl are common from April through October and are easily viewed from boardwalk platforms. Dawn and dusk are the best times to see white-tailed deer browsing and grazing.

Directions: *From Route 128, take Route 1A north for 8.3 miles to Ipswich South Village Green. Turn right on Route 133 and follow it for 1.5 miles to a left turn on Northgate Road. Follow Northgate to its end and turn right on Argilla Road to the gate and parking area.*

Ownership: TTOR (508) 356-4351

Size: 1,400 acres   **Closest Town:** Ipswich

41. IPSWICH RIVER WILDLIFE SANCTUARY

Description: The open grasslands of the Ipswich River floodplain are rich in nutrients that attract wetland wildlife and migratory birds. Names like Teal Pond and Waterfowl Pond suggest the area has long been used by ducks and water birds.

Viewing Information: Beavers play an active role in the floodplain ecology of this site. Water impounded by beaver dams creates extensive wetlands by trapping spring meltwater. As the water recedes, small vernal pools are left. These pools are important amphibian breeding sites. Blue- and green-winged teal, mergansers, great blue herons, and snowy egrets feed in the river's shallows. Song sparrows, common yellowthroats, and red-winged blackbirds are found along wetland edges. The flat, meandering river can be seen from the boardwalk and observation tower. A staffed visitor center provides a comprehensive introduction to the property, and interpretive walks are regularly scheduled. The sanctuary is closed Mondays.

Directions: *From Interstate 95, take Route 1 north. Turn right on Route 97 at the traffic light. Take the second left off Route 97 on Perkins Row. The site entrance is 1 mile on the right.*

Ownership: MAS (508) 887-9264

Size: 2,267 acres   **Closest Town:** Topsfield

42. DELANEY WILDLIFE MANAGEMENT AREA

Description: Three small flood control dams create a shallow, stumpy, 100-acre impoundment and two open marshes dominated by buttonbush, smartweed, and cattails. Several fields are maintained, but the remainder of the upland has reverted to second-growth white pine forest.

Viewing Information: Scan the pond from the boat ramp parking lot or from the top of the earthen dam. Wood ducks use natural nesting cavities in trees in addition to wooden nest boxes mounted on posts in the wetlands. A canoe is a good way to explore the pond for amphibians, painted turtles, largemouth bass, pickerels, and panfish. Four and a half miles of unmarked trails provide access to pine stands and open fields. Waterfowl blinds are available for wildlife observation except during waterfowl hunting season. Contact the DFW office at the number below for details.

Directions: *From Route 495, take Route 117 east for 3.2 miles to Harvard Road. Turn left and travel 1.4 miles to the parking lot on the left.*

Ownership: DFW (508) 263-4347

Size: 560 acres   **Closest Town:** Stow

Description: The refuge office and visitor center sits at the base of a 12,000-year-old glacial deposit known as Weir Hill. The hill was once home to Native Americans who constructed fish traps, or weirs, in the adjacent Sudbury River. Today, 12 miles of the Concord and Sudbury rivers and their associated uplands and wetlands constitute the refuge. Migratory birds, especially waterfowl, find the habitat ideal for nesting or for stopovers during migration.

Viewing Information: Weir Hill offers more than a mile of trails through woodlands, fields, and along the river and wetlands. Muskrats and red foxes are common. Reptiles and amphibians can be seen around wetland edges during warmer months. The northern parcel features the 1.7-mile Dike Trail, where a photo blind and an observation tower offer unique views of wood ducks, blue-winged teal, and great blue herons. Wood duck boxes dot the wetlands and provide nesting cavities for "woodies," hooded mergansers, and tree swallows.

Directions: *From Route 20 in Wayland, take Route 27 north for 1.7 miles and turn right on Water Row Road. Continue for 1.2 miles to the road's end and turn right on Lincoln Road. Stay on Lincoln for one-half mile and turn left onto Weir Hill Road.*

Ownership: USFWS (508) 443-4661

Size: 3,400 acres   **Closest Town:** Sudbury

A male marsh wren sings during courtship to attract a passing female, hoping to entice her to one of several prospective nests he has constructed nearby. Great Meadows National Wildlife Refuge is one of the few sites in Massachusetts where this species breeds.
BILL BYRNE

NORTHEAST

Description: Drumlin Farm features sustainable agriculture exhibits and a large collection of native species on display in naturally landscaped enclosures. More than 100 acres of pasture, fields, and woodlands are managed to provide diverse wildlife habitat.

Viewing Information: Leave the hustle and bustle of nearby Route 128 and the high-tech industry behind and enjoy the suburban open space of Drumlin Farm. Live animal exhibits afford a chance for extended and detailed wildlife observation and photography. Staff give excellent natural history presentations indoors and out, tailored to changes in the seasons and the dynamics of wild-life populations. Trails cover the grounds and pass plantings of wildflowers, ornamental trees, and shrubs, which attract migrating warblers and resident chickadees, house finches, tufted titmice, and chipping sparrows. The Audubon gift shop contains a wealth of books and information on birding, bird conservation, and environmental issues of concern at the local, national, and global level. The sanctuary is closed Mondays.

Directions: *From Route 128, take Route 117 west for 4.5 miles to the entrance. From Route 495, take Route 117 east for approximately 13 miles to the intersection of routes 117 and 126. Continue east on Route 117 for 0.7 mile to the entrance.*

Ownership: MAS (617) 259-9807

Size: 256 acres   **Closest Town:** Lincoln

A member of the neotropical migrant group, the rose-breasted grosbeak nests in northern latitudes and winters in the tropics. Its heavy beak enables it to take advantage of a diverse seasonal diet of insects, fruits, and seeds.
BILL BYRNE

45. BELLE ISLE MARSH RESERVATION

Description: The Belle Isle Marsh is a remnant of the wetland habitat that dominated much of the Boston Harbor shoreline in precolonial times. Now an urban oasis, the marsh provides open space for wildlife and people alike.

Viewing Information: The rich layers of decaying marsh vegetation provide nutrients at the base of the food chain. Invertebrates such as crustaceans and shellfish feed on microorganisms and are in turn fed upon by fish, birds, and mammals. Birds are Belle Isle's most conspicuous inhabitants, particularly the herons and egrets. Twenty-seven species of shorebirds and eleven species of hawks have been recorded here. The 28 acres of landscaped park provide pathways, benches, and an observation tower affording views over the marsh and of Boston Harbor beyond.

Directions: *From Route 1A north, take the second exit for Winthrop/Chelsea onto Bennington Street. Continue approximately 1.5 miles to the main entrance on the right. From Route 1A south, turn left on Boardman Street to Bennington Street. Turn left on Bennington and follow it for 0.5 mile to the entrance on the right. Also accessible via mass transit by taking the MBTA Blue Line to Suffolk Downs Station.*

Ownership: MDC (617) 727-5350

Size: 175 acres   **Closest City:** Boston

Snowy egrets nest in association with other colonial waterbirds on some of Massachusetts' coastal islands and disperse to areas like Belle Isle Marsh Reservation after the breeding season. Watch for egrets hunting in shallow, tidal waters.
BILL BYRNE

NORTHEAST

71

Description: Six of Boston Harbor's islands are managed cooperatively to provide open space, recreation, and education on cultural and natural history subjects. Open seasonally, the islands have colorful histories ranging from pirates and shipwrecks to forts and prison camps. The habitat is as varied as the history, with tidal pools, flats, salt marshes, a freshwater pond, and tree-covered uplands.

Viewing Information: Ferry service is available to George's Island, which serves as the gateway to Harbor Islands State Park. Water taxis provide access to the neighboring islands free of charge. Waterfowl and gulls find the harbor and island shorelines prime habitat. Small mammals, particularly rabbits, favor the grassy interiors and old structures. Herons, egrets, and ibises frequent the flats and marshes, hunting fish and crustaceans in tidal waters. Spectacular views of Boston Harbor and the Boston skyline are found on all islands. Contact Bay State Cruises for seasonal ferry schedule and departure points (617) 723-7800. Ferries most often run from Long Wharf in Boston and Hewitt's Cove in Hingham. Limited dock space for private boats is available on George's Island on a first-come first-served basis.

Ownership: MDC & DEM (617) 727-7676

Size: 419 acres   **Closest City:** Boston

American oystercatchers are increasing in number along the coast. Their long, orange bills and shrill, whistling call make them one of the most conspicuous birds on the beach.
BILL BYRNE

Description: Stately hardwood trees line gently curving carriage paths that traverse low glacial hills. The hills reach into Hingham Bay at the mouth of the Weir River, providing panoramic views with Boston Harbor as a backdrop. Sloping meadows dominate the main hills while red cedar and blueberry thickets cover the granite outcrops of Rocky Neck.

Viewing Information: Seven miles of carriage paths and footpaths lead wildlife viewers past salt and brackish marshes, rocky overlooks, and the top of Planter's Hill. Migrant songbirds, traveling along the coast, find sanctuary in undeveloped fields and woodlands and are watched by keen-eyed predators like sharp-shinned and Cooper's hawks. Merlins and American kestrels, both falcons, also hunt the fields. In winter, sea ducks group in numbers off the rugged shoreline. Herons and egrets prowl the marshes, searching for finfish and crabs.

Directions: *From Route 3, take exit 14 for Route 228. Follow Route 228 north for 6.5 miles, turn left on Route 3A, and follow it for 0.5 mile to Summer Street on the right. Take Summer Street 0.3 mile to Rockland Street at the traffic light. Cross Rockland Street and follow Martin's Lane 0.7 mile to the entrance.*

Ownership: TTOR (617) 749-8956

Size: 251 acres   **Closest Town:** Hingham

Marshes with low, woody vegetation are favored by the green heron. This crow-sized wading bird builds a loosely-woven stick nest low in a thicket It searches the shallows for fish, amphibians, and invertebrates.
BILL BYRNE

NORTHEAST

73

Description: A functional solar-heated visitor center is one aspect of the wide-ranging environmental education agenda promoted at Broadmoor. In addition to the exhibits and programs available, wildlife viewing options at the site focus on vast wetlands interspersed with fields and woodlands.

Viewing Information: Resident Canada geese and mallards are regularly seen in the wetlands, often with broods of young in the spring. Snapping turtles are present and can prey on goslings and ducklings, striking from below and pulling the young birds underwater. Listen for gray catbirds and yellow warblers calling from dense wetland vegetation; look for the dark-feathered cap of the catbird and delicate chestnut streaking on the sides of the warbler. A variety of nesting boxes have been erected to attract everything from wood ducks and grackles to bluebirds and house wrens. The sanctuary is closed Mondays.

Directions: *From Boston, take the Massachusetts Turnpike (Interstate 90) west to exit 16. Take Route 16 west for about 7 miles to South Natick. Stay on Route 16 for 1.8 miles beyond the center of town to the site entrance on the left. From the west, take Route 9 east to Route 27 south. At the intersection of routes 27 and 16, turn left on Route 16. After crossing the Natick town line, look for the site entrance on the right.*

Ownership: MAS (508) 655-2296

Size: 623 acres   **Closest Towns:** Sherborn and Natick

Fruit-bearing trees like crabapples will attract cedar waxwings from late summer into early winter. The waxwings' high-pitched call can be heard overhead in spring and summer as they search the treetops for insects.
BILL BYRNE

Description: Great Blue Hill rises 635 feet above the coastal plain, offering spectacular views in every season. The surrounding 7,000 acres of rocky hilltops, oak and pine woodlands, red maple swamps, wet meadows, and Atlantic white cedar bog form the largest tract of open space within 35 miles of Boston. The Trailside Museum, operated by the Massachusetts Audubon Society, offers exhibits and public programs describing the reservation's history.

Viewing Information: The Trailside Museum provides an excellent introduction to the wildlife of the Blue Hills through live native animal exhibits. White-tailed deer, a variety of hawks and owls, and the secretive timber rattlesnake can be viewed closely and safely. The 125-mile trail system crisscrosses habitat attractive to hermit thrushes, winter wrens, and kingfishers. Turkey vultures ride thermal currents and updrafts created by the hills. Eastern coyotes and red foxes hunt meadow voles and cottontail rabbits throughout the year, adding blueberries and wild grapes to their diet in the summer and fall.

Directions: *For Trailside Museum: from Route 128 (Interstate 93), take exit 2B, Route 138, Milton. Travel north on Route 138 for 0.5 mile to the museum parking area on the right. For Blue Hills Reservation: take exit 3 and follow the signs for Houghtons Pond. Turn right at the first stop sign. The reservation headquarters is 0.5 mile on the left, located between the state police stable and station.*

Ownership: MDC (617) 698-1802; Trailside Museum information (617) 333-0690

Size: 7,000 acres   **Closest Town:** Milton

Eastern coyotes are more often heard than seen, as family groups communicate using barks, yips, and howls. Coyotes are found statewide and have successfully colonized suburban habitat, testimony to their tremendous adaptability. Their diet can include large and small mammals, carrion, fruit, birds, and amphibians. BILL BYRNE

NORTHEAST

50. MOOSE HILL WILDLIFE SANCTUARY

Description: Moose Hill is one of the jewels of open space found in the greater Boston area. The extensive red maple swamp provides habitat for amphibians, birds, and a host of invertebrates. Walks are led by sanctuary naturalists who describe the ecology of the site and the interrelationships between wildlife, vegetation, the land, and people.

Viewing Information: A quarter-mile boardwalk through a red maple swamp invites you into a unique habitat without damaging it. Dragonflies hunt mosquitoes over pockets of open water while spiders take a more passive approach to obtaining a meal, waiting in gossamer webs for a victim to appear. Listen for the vocalizations of wood frogs and gray tree frogs and patiently use your binoculars to look for individual animals at close range. Broad-winged hawks are found on the upland sections of the property. Dense thickets of low vegetation provide cover for mockingbirds and cardinals. Maps and other information are available at the visitor center. The sanctuary is closed Mondays.

Directions: From Interstate 95 south, take exit 10 and turn left at the end of the ramp. At the intersection with Route 27, turn right toward Walpole. Stay on Route 27 for 0.5 mile then turn left on Moose Hill Street and travel 1.5 miles to the parking area on the left.

Ownership: MAS (617) 784-5691

Size: 1,975 acres   **Closest Town:** Sharon

Best known for its ability to mimic or "mock" other birds' calls, the mockingbird is often found in open areas near shrubs and brush and will aggressively defend its nesting and feeding territory. Mockingbirds can be incessant singers, often vocalizing well into the night. BILL BYRNE

51. BRISTOL-BLAKE STATE RESERVATION & STONY BROOK WILDLIFE SANCTUARY

Description: A combination of open water, wetlands, and woodlands provides a habitat mix attractive to aquatic and terrestrial wildlife alike. Waterfowl are drawn to Stony Brook Pond, where a boardwalk affords prime access and open views. The surrounding wetlands, wooded swamp, meadow, and oak/pine uplands host an array of reptiles, amphibians, birds, and mammals.

Viewing Information: The Stony Brook Visitor Center has information on current viewing opportunities. The boardwalk takes you to the wetland, where male red-winged blackbirds make their springtime "conk-a-ree" call. Common grackles, bluebirds, and tree swallows are present as well. The marsh edges are favorite hunting areas for great blue and green herons. On open water, resident Canada geese watch over their goslings, while mallards, black ducks, and wood ducks arrive and depart on the wing. Don't overlook the waters under and beside the boardwalk; the structure and its shade provide cover for bluegills and bass. Check the boardwalk posts just above the water line for the shed "skin" of dragonfly larvae. The skins are left when the developed dragonfly emerges to begin life in the air.

Directions: *From Interstate 495, take Route 1A north through Wrentham to the intersection with Route 115. Turn left on Route 115 and follow it for 1.5 miles to North Street and turn left. The site entrance is on the right.*

Ownership: DEM/MAS (508) 528-3140

Size: 241 acres   **Closest Town:** Norfolk

NORTHEAST

Canada geese are found throughout the year in Massachusetts wherever a food source exists in close proximity to open water. These resident birds are non-migratory and are a separate population from the flocks of geese seen passing high overhead in V-formation. Local concentrations of geese have caused problems on beaches, golf courses, playing fields, and reservoirs. BILL BYRNE

SOUTHEAST REGION—COASTAL PLAIN, CAPE COD, AND THE ISLANDS

Sandy beaches, rolling surf, and pitch pine forests are the images many people associate with southeastern Massachusetts. The beaches and sandy soils are the result of the retreating glaciers and the effects of wind and water on the till and outwash left behind. In places, up to 400 feet of sand, gravel, and clay cover the bedrock. Coastal plain ponds, saltwater and freshwater marshes, and mixed forests with dense understory add to the habitat diversity. The Taunton River flows across the coastal plain to Mount Hope Bay and is influenced by tides well upstream from its mouth. Cape Cod is etched by small, clear rivers feeding nutrient-rich estuaries where aquatic and terrestrial wildlife thrive. Sixteen wildlife viewing sites are found in the region. Stellwagen Bank, the offshore marine sanctuary featured on the cover of this guide, is one of the jewels.

Watching a December sunset from a Martha's Vineyard beach (Site 60) can be a very solitary experience. Visiting this region in the "off season" will provide more room to roam and time to experience the natural beauty of southeastern Massachusetts.
BILL BYRNE

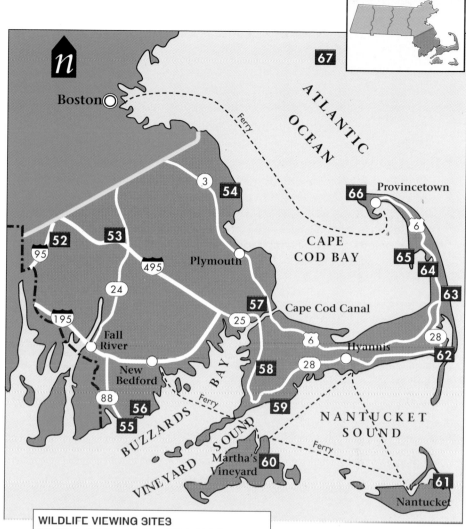

WILDLIFE VIEWING SITES

52. North Attleboro National Fish Hatchery
53. Hockomock Swamp and Erwin S. Wilder Wildlife Management Areas
54. Daniel Webster Wildlife Sanctuary
55. Horseneck Beach State Reservation
56. Lloyd Center for Environmental Studies and Demarest Lloyd State Park
57. Cape Cod Canal and Scusset Beach State Reservation
58. Crane Wildlife Management Area
59. South Cape Beach State Park
60. Martha's Vineyard Group
61. Nantucket Refuge Group
62. Monomoy National Wildlife Refuge
63. Nauset Marsh and Fort Hill—Cape Cod National Seashore
64. Wellfleet Bay Wildlife Sanctuary
65. Great Island—Cape Cod National Seashore
66. Race Point—Cape Cod National Seashore
67. Stellwagen Bank National Marine Sanctuary

Description: Designed for rearing Atlantic salmon, the North Attleboro National Fish Hatchery offers ponds, wetlands, a nature trail, and barrier-free trout fishing and viewing pools.

Viewing Information: An Atlantic salmon display pool and a 0.8-mile nature trail are open daily. Group tours of the facility are available with reservations. In addition to cultured trout and salmon, waterfowl and great blue herons are regularly seen.

Directions: *From Interstate 495, take exit 14B for Route 1 south. Turn left at the first traffic light onto Route 152 and follow it to Bungay Road on the left. Take Bungay Road 0.3 mile to the hatchery entrance on the left.*

Ownership: USFWS (508) 695-5002

Size: 223 acres   **Closest Town:** North Attleboro

A drake hooded merganser stretches his wings. These small cavity-nesting ducks lay their eggs in wood duck nest boxes and natural sites near fresh water. The long, thin, serrated bill helps them catch fish, crustaceans, and aquatic insects. BILL BYRNE

Description: Vast shrub, cedar, and red maple swamps spread out across the flat landscape, broken by small, meandering rivers, wooded uplands, an abandoned railroad grade, a power line right-of-way, and maintained agricultural fields. Lake Nippenicket has a long, undeveloped shoreline and boat ramp for wildlife watchers wishing to view the site from a canoe or shallow-draft power boat.

Viewing Information: On foot or by canoe, wildlife watchers exploring the west shoreline of Lake Nippenicket will find a vegetated swamp and forested uplands. A cart road skirts a cedar swamp, where pitcher plants are found. Hemlock and beech trees shelter red and gray squirrels, rabbits, red foxes, and white-tailed deer. Muskrats swim among the buttonbush. Just west of the lake, a 1.5-mile road at the end of Hall Street is blocked to vehicles, creating excellent access to the interior of the property. Follow the roadway through the swamp to the power line right-of-way. The swamp harbors spotted and painted turtles and a variety of amphibians, while dry sections of the right-of-way are prime habitat for red-tailed hawks, American kestrels, and hog-nosed snakes.

Directions: *For Hockomock and Lake Nippenicket: from Interstate 495, take Route 24 north to Route 104 west. Boat ramp is just off the interchange on the right. Continue on Route 104 west to Elm Street. Turn right on Elm and follow it for 0.5 mile to Chase Road or 1 mile to Hall Street, both on the right, for trail and roadway walks. For Wilder: from I-495, take the Bay Street exit. Follow Bay Street north for 0.5 mile to Toad Island Road on the right.*

Ownership: DFW (508) 759-3406

Size: 5,450 acres   **Closest Town:** Raynham

Muskrats are found in both fresh and brackish water, where they build dome-shaped "houses" using marsh vegetation. BILL BYRNE

Description: Daniel Webster comprises more than 300 acres of grasslands and 150 acres of woodlands. The resulting edge effect is ideal for small mammals and the raptors that prey upon them. The Green Harbor River forms the northern border of the property, and the associated tidal areas are home to a variety of water birds.

Viewing Information: Red-tailed hawks hunt by day and great horned owls hunt by night for mice and voles in the grasslands. Ospreys fish the river and American kestrels scan their surroundings from conspicuous perches. Listen for secretive rails calling during the warmer months from the flooded grasses. Tree swallows catch flying insects on the wing and use natural cavities and manmade boxes for nest sites. More than 1,000 feet of boardwalks and two wildlife observation blinds provide access to wetlands. In winter, northern harriers, rough-legged hawks, and short-eared owls can be seen flying low over the grasses. Long-distance glimpses of red foxes or eastern coyotes are possible at any time of year. The Daniel Webster Sanctuary is a featured attraction among the South Shore Sanctuaries network. Information on other nearby sites is available from the North River Sanctuary office (617) 837-9400. The sanctuary is closed Mondays.

Directions: *From Route 3 south, take exit 12 for Route 139 toward Marshfield. In Marshfield, turn right on Webster Street and follow it for 1.4 miles. Then turn left on Winslow Cemetery Road. The site entrance is at the road's end.*

Ownership: MAS (617) 837-9400

Size: 431 acres   **Closest Town:** Marshfield

A great horned owl zeroes in on a small mammal using its acute senses of sight and hearing. These owls are nocturnal predators capable of taking prey as large as a striped skunk. Listen for their deep hoots in the pre-dawn darkness.
BILL BYRNE

Description: An extensive beach overlooking Rhode Island Sound provides seasonal habitat for shore birds and water birds. The rich waters of the Westport Rivers support shellfish, finfish, and a dense population of nesting ospreys.

Viewing Information: Spring and fall are prime viewing seasons. Ospreys reclaim their nests in April and shore birds and waterfowl are most conspicuous during fall migrations. Ospreys use low nesting platforms that dot the salt marsh and islands of the Westport Rivers. The females can be seen atop the large, bulky stick nests; the males are often perched nearby. Watch ospreys hover over open water as they prepare to plunge, feet first, into the shallows to catch a winter flounder or alewife. Dunlins favor exposed flats. Ruddy turnstones and purple sandpipers flock along the rocky edges of Gooseberry Neck. Paved pathways, the Tabor Point Trail, or the shoreline at low tide offer multiple vantage points.

Directions: *From Interstate 195, take Route 88 south for 12 miles to John Reed Road. Osprey nests and the Westport River will be on your left and the beach entrance will be on your right.*

Ownership: DEM (508) 636-8816

Size: 537 acres   **Closest Town:** Westport

Ospreys have recovered from a population low of 11 nesting pairs in Massachusetts in the early 1960s to more than 300 pairs today. This young osprey was photographed when it was leg-banded in the nest. The bands provide vital information on migration, dispersal, and mortality. BILL BYRNE

SOUTHEAST

83

56. LLOYD CENTER FOR ENVIRONMENTAL STUDIES AND DEMAREST LLOYD STATE PARK

Description: A 100-year-old oak/hickory forest meets the sea at the Slocums River estuary. An extensive visitor center with an observation deck makes the Lloyd Center an exceptional viewing and educational site. The larger, unstaffed Demarest Lloyd State Park adds a freshwater marsh, salt marsh, brackish pond, maritime forest, sandy beach, and additional river frontage to the habitat mix.

Viewing Information: Enjoy views of the Slocums River, Buzzards Bay, and the Elizabeth Islands from the Lloyd Center's top floor observation deck, where up to 75 species of birds have been seen during a single day. Stop at the butterfly garden for a glimpse of a spicebush swallowtail or ruby-throated hummingbird. Take a leisurely walk on one of several trails through the oak/hickory forest, to the salt marsh, or to the kettle pond, where an observation blind awaits. Harbor seals, common loons, and a variety of diving ducks are winter regulars within the estuary. At nearby Demarest Lloyd State Park, check salt marsh and beach margins for greater yellowlegs, willets, snowy egrets, and green crabs. Goldfinches and purple finches are year-round residents. Colorful warblers can be seen gleaning insects in the forest canopy during spring and fall migrations.

Directions: *From Interstate 195, take exit 12 and head south toward North Dartmouth. Cross Route 6 and continue 0.25 mile to a fork in the road. Bear left on Chase Road and follow it to its end. Turn right on Russells Mills Road, drive 0.9 mile, and turn left on Rock O' Dundee Road. Drive 0.9 mile to Potomska Road, turn right, and continue to the entrance 1.7 miles on right.*

Ownership: Lloyd Center for Environmental Studies (508) 990-0505; DEM (508) 636-8816

Size: Lloyd Center, 55 acres; Demarest Lloyd State Park, 222 acres

Closest Town: Dartmouth

Introduced from Europe to add elegance and beauty to parks and estates, mute swans are now established in the wild. These huge birds can be aggressive during the nesting season, striking with their bill and wings.
BILL BYRNE

57. CAPE COD CANAL AND SCUSSET BEACH STATE RESERVATION

Description: The Cape Cod Canal is referred to as the Gateway to Cape Cod. Scusset Beach provides recreation and wildlife viewing at the canal's east end.

Viewing Information: From April to June, the Cape Cod Canal's Bournedale Herring Run is used by thousands of alewives on their spawning migration to Great Herring Pond. Striped bass and bluefish can be seen chasing alewives in the canal near the base of the run as black-backed and herring gulls circle overhead. Herring can be viewed in the run as they head upstream. A paved pathway allows for easy walking or bicycling along the canal's edge. In winter, the waters off Scusset Beach and the adjoining Sandcatcher Recreation Area host common eiders and goldeneyes, red-breasted mergansers, common loons, and harbor seals. *USE CAUTION ON THE SANDCATCHER BREAKWATER; WAVES CAN COME OVER THE TOP DURING STORMY CONDITIONS.* Mowed fields are used by horned larks and fast-flying merlins hunting the open spaces from above.

Directions: *From Route 495, follow Route 25 south to the Route 6 east exit BEFORE the Bourne Bridge over the canal. Follow Route 6 as it parallels the canal to the Bournedale Herring Run Recreation Area on your right. To Scusset Beach, continue on Route 6 to the Sagamore Bridge traffic circle. Proceed halfway around the circle to the Scusset Beach signs. Follow the signs for 1.5 miles to the entrance.*

Ownership: Bournedale Herring Run, USACE (508) 759-4431; Scusset Beach Reservation, DEM (508) 888-0859

Size: 380 acres   **Closest Town:** Bourne

Early in the 1900s herring gulls were considered rare in Massachusetts and a sanctuary was acquired in Buzzards Bay to provide nesting habitat. Now, some 15,000 to 20,000 pairs nest along the coast, having exploited new food sources found in association with landfills and the commercial fishing industry.
BILL BYRNE

SOUTHEAST

85

Description: Pitch pine scrub oak woodlands give way to open, grassy fields bordered by dense hedgerows. The dry, sandy soils and related forest type are typical of interior Cape Cod.

Viewing·Information: Bobwhite quail and ring-necked pheasants favor fields and hedgerows, often staying under impenetrable thickets of multiflora rose and autumn olive to avoid detection by red foxes, red-tailed hawks, and great horned owls. Songbirds take advantage of the edges of fields and forest for food, shelter, and nesting sites. Mockingbirds, robins, bluebirds, tufted titmice, and cardinals are commonly seen. Woodchucks create den sites by burrowing under the root systems of dense vegetation. Freshly excavated soil can be seen around multiple entrances when a den is actively being used. White-tailed deer are regularly encountered.

Directions: *From Route 495 south, follow Route 25 south and cross the Cape Cod Canal via the Bourne Bridge. From the rotary on the far side of the bridge, follow Route 28 east to Route 151 east. Several entrances to the site are found on the left side of Route 151 from 1 to 3 miles from the Route 28 interchange.*

Ownership: DFW (508) 759-3406

Size: 1,700 acres   **Closest Town:** Mashpee

Snow, mud, sand, and even wet grass can reveal wildlife tracks and sign, adding a new dimension to the viewing experience. Ring-necked pheasant and cottontail rabbit tracks are evident here in new-fallen snow. Note the long drag marks made by the pheasant's tail and toe and the cottontail's interest in the exposed vegetation.
BILL BYRNE

Description: As part of the Waquoit Bay National Estuarine Research Reserve, South Cape Beach offers a full range of marine and intertidal habitats from coastal beach, estuary, and salt pond to dune, salt marsh, and pitch pine uplands. The open waters of Nantucket Sound contrast with sheltered Waquoit Bay, Sage Lot Pond, and Flat Pond, offering a variety of viewing opportunities year-round.

Viewing Information: The South Cape Beach trails provide good views of Sage Lot and Flat Ponds, and of the beach and dunes. Snowy egrets and green herons stalk the pond's shallows and ospreys nest on poles along the far shoreline. The wet sand and high-tide line along the beach are favored feeding habitat for piping plovers and sanderlings. Take the Flat Pond Trail and scan the pond for mute swans and great black-backed gulls. Use the boardwalk and watch the dune grass for savannah and song sparrows or horned larks in exposed openings. Over open water, laughing gulls and least terns attempt to catch schooling American sand lance and alewives.

Directions: *From the rotary at routes 28 and 151 in Mashpee, follow Route 28 west toward Falmouth for 1.5 miles to Red Brook Road. Turn left on Red Brook Road and follow it to a stop sign. Take a sharp right on Great Oak Road. Beach parking is 1.5 miles on the left.*

Ownership: DEM (508) 457-0495

Size: 450 acres   **Closest Town:** Mashpee

Piping plovers are increasing in numbers due, in part, to proactive beach management policies which protect plovers and their habitat. Here, a male plover does his own "beach management" by escorting an intruder out of the territory while his mate sits on a clutch of eggs nearby.
BILL BYRNE

SOUTHEAST

Description: Multiple conservation lands dot the Martha's Vineyard landscape with the 5,300-acre Manuel Corellus State Forest dominating the interior. A number of pine and oak forests, grasslands, heathlands, dunes, wetlands, and beaches are accessible by foot, bicycle, or motor vehicle, offering many views of the island's ecosystems.

Viewing Information: Maps and general island information are available near the Vineyard Haven ferry dock. The Felix Neck Wildlife Sanctuary is open year-round and is an excellent starting point. Ospreys and barn owls are featured sanctuary attractions during the nesting season, and an observation blind is available for waterfowl watchers. Interpretive programs are offered regularly. At Corellus State Forest, a 12-mile paved bicycle trail winds through extensive pine and oak stands occupied by songbirds, gamebirds, white-tailed deer, and a variety of small mammals. On the Vineyard's south and east shores, the Long Point, Wasque, and Cape Poge Wildlife Refuges contain sand plain grasslands, heath, and long stretches of open beach. Northern harriers and red-tailed hawks fly low over the huckleberry and seaside goldenrod thickets in search of prey. Shorebirds are conspicuous along beaches during both migration and the nesting season. Monarch and swallowtail butterflies are commonplace in open uplands throughout the summer.

Directions: *Follow Route 495 south to Route 25 south to Route 28 east at Bourne Bridge. Cross the bridge and stay on Route 28 to signs for Woods Hole ferry. Take the ferry to Vineyard Haven dock. Then take Edgartown Road for 4 miles to the Felix Neck Sanctuary entrance on the left. Steamship Authority (ferry) (508) 477-8600.*

Ownership: Felix Neck Sanctuary, MAS (508) 627-4850; Manuel Corellus State Forest, DEM (508) 693-2540; Long Point, Wasque, Cape Poge Refuges, TTOR (508) 693-3678

Size: 6,841 acres (combined)   **Closest Towns:** Tisbury & Edgartown

Floating a river, stream, lake, pond, or coastal area is a great way to watch wildlife. Canoes and small boats are effective ways to access remote areas and backwaters.

At Edgartown Light on Martha's Vineyard, sunrise brings increased wildlife activity and new chances for wildlife viewing and photography. BILL BYRNE

61. NANTUCKET REFUGE GROUP

Description: The northern tip of Nantucket juts 5 miles into the Atlantic Ocean, forming Great Point. The resulting barrier beach shelters Nantucket Sound, the Harbor, and Coatue Point from fierce winter storms. More than 21 miles of shoreline and 1,300 acres of land are preserved by public and private conservation organizations at this site. Wind sculpts the sand and vegetation, creating dynamic beaches and dunes and stunted thickets of oak and cedar. Elsewhere on Nantucket, an additional 11,000 acres are available to wildlife watchers; a variety of public agencies and private groups combine to protect open space and a diversity of habitats.

Viewing Information: Access to the site is via the Wauwinet Gatehouse. Pedestrians and four-wheel-drive over-sand vehicles (with restrictions) are permitted. *HIKING OVER SOFT SAND IS DEMANDING. THERE ARE NO FACILITIES WITHIN THE REFUGES. KNOW YOUR LIMITATIONS.* Nantucket Harbor is rich with waterfowl and shellfish. Dabbling ducks and Canada geese are present year-round. Sea ducks, such as eiders, scoters, oldsquaws, and scaups assemble offshore in winter. Greater yellowlegs, willets, and whimbrels can be heard and seen flying low along the shoreline. Several sections of beach are important nesting and feeding sites for piping plovers and least terns. Look for the tracks of shorebirds and gulls in damp beach sand just above the reach of the waves. Striped bass and bluefish are found near shore on both the Nantucket Sound and Atlantic Ocean sides of the beach from spring through fall. Watch for baitfish near the surface, responding to the predatory fish below, and look for birds attracted by the baitfish.

Directions: *From Route 6 on Cape Cod, take Route 132 to Hyannis. Follow signs for Steamship Authority ferry to Nantucket. From the village of Nantucket, take Orange Street around the rotary to Milestone Road. Take the second left off Milestone Road to Polpis Road and follow it approximately 4.5 miles to a left turn on Wauwinet Road to the gatehouse at the end. Steamship Authority (ferry) (508) 477-8600.*

Ownership: Coskata-Coatue Wildlife Refuge, TTOR (508) 921-1944; Coatue/ Haulover Wildlife Refuge, Nantucket Conservation Foundation (508) 228-2884; Nantucket National Wildlife Refuge, USFWS (508) 443-4661

Size: 1,308 acres (combined)   **Closest Town:** Nantucket

Owing to modern wildlife management practices, there are likely more white-tailed deer in Massachusetts today than when the Pilgrims landed in Plymouth in 1620.

Description: Monomoy is the only federally designated wilderness area in Massachusetts, and as such is left in its natural state to be "affected primarily by the forces of nature." Currently comprising two barrier islands and surrounding tidal flats, Monomoy's sandy surface is constantly shifting and changing under the unrelenting actions of winds and waves.

Viewing Information: Shorebirds and water birds are the feature attraction from spring through fall. Monomoy is an important stopover point for migrating greater yellowlegs, willets, red knots, and least and pectoral sandpipers. In summer, great black-backed and herring gulls nest by the thousands among the low vegetation while least, common, and roseate terns occupy more exposed areas above the reach of the tides. Black skimmers are seen on the periphery of the islands, and occasionally they nest here. Peregrine falcons appear regularly in the fall, cruising low over the beaches on their southward journey. Winter brings more than 1,000 harbor and gray seals. A growing number of seals linger and have pups on the beaches of Monomoy, the southernmost breeding site in eastern North America for these marine mammals. The refuge office is accessible by car, but a boat is necessary to reach the islands. Local charter boats are available to ferry wildlife watchers to Monomoy. Organized tours are scheduled seasonally.

Directions: *From Route 6, take Route 137 south to Route 28 in Chatham. Follow Route 28 east and turn right on Stage Harbor Road. Continue to Bridge Street, turn left, and continue to Morris Island Road on the right. Follow Morris Island Road to the refuge office.*

Ownership: USFWS (508) 443-4661

Size: 2,750 acres   **Closest Town:** Chatham

SOUTHEAST

A least tern returns from a fishing trip with a meal for its chicks. About 2,500 pairs of least terns nest at 55 sites along the Bay State coast. BILL BYRNE

91

63. NAUSET MARSH & FORT HILL— CAPE COD NATIONAL SEASHORE

Description: Nauset Marsh is protected from the Atlantic Ocean by Nauset and Coast Guard Beaches. The beach habitat is home to nesting and migrating shorebirds. Behind the beach, the nutrient-rich salt marsh functions as a nursery for marine life from microscopic plankton to prized sport fish.

Viewing Information: Fort Hill offers an impressive view of Nauset Marsh with Coast Guard Beach and the Atlantic Ocean providing a backdrop. Use binoculars or a spotting scope to scan the marsh edges and creeks for wading great blue herons or black-crowned night herons. Look for osprey nesting poles out on the marsh with birds in residence from April through August. The Fort Hill Trail passes along the thick upland understory where red foxes and cottontail rabbits can be found. A short drive to the Salt Pond Visitor Center provides access to the Nauset Marsh Trail and a second scenic overlook. Enjoy walking among the beach plum, black cherry, bayberry, and pitch pine, and listen for the distinctive "bobwhite" call of quail. At Salt Pond, mussels and quahogs can be found. A short distance beyond, Coast Guard Beach provides nesting habitat for piping plovers and least terns and feeding grounds for migrating sandpipers, dunlins, and dowitchers. Information and an interpretive trail are available at Salt Pond Visitor Center.

Directions: *Traveling east on Route 6 in Eastham, look for signs for Fort Hill on your right. Salt Pond Visitor Center is just over a mile farther east on Route 6.*

Ownership: NPS (508) 349-3785

Size: 2,265 acres   **Closest Town:** Eastham

Cottontails and other small mammals are a staple in the diets of coyotes, hawks, and owls. Predator populations shadow prey species' populations, alternately rising and falling in long-term cycles.
BILL BYRNE

64. WELLFLEET BAY WILDLIFE SANCTUARY

Description: A new visitor center greets wildlife watchers at Wellfleet Bay, providing insight into the marine and terrestrial environments of Cape Cod. Uplands forested by pitch pine and scrub oak border an expansive salt marsh and the bay itself. A boardwalk offers excellent views of the coastal habitats.

Viewing Information: The fertile waters and tidal flats of Wellfleet Bay and the surrounding salt marshes draw thousands of migrating shorebirds and waterfowl in the spring and fall. Flocks of dunlins, sanderlings, and least sandpipers feed on invertebrates exposed by falling tides and wave action. Diving ducks, including scaups and mergansers, raft and feed in open water. Seed- and insect-eating birds find the pine and oak stands to their liking. Chickadees and nuthatches hastily probe branches, cones, and the bark of pines in search of seeds and insect larvae. The forest floor and the neighboring fields are habitat for long-lived eastern box turtles. The sanctuary is closed Mondays.

Directions: *From Route 6 east, turn left at the site entrance located just north of the Eastham/Wellfleet town line.*

Ownership: MAS (508) 349-2615

Size: 838 acres   **Closest Town:** Eastham

65. GREAT ISLAND—CAPE COD NATIONAL SEASHORE

Description: There are few spots on mainland Cape Cod farther from a paved road than the Jeremy Point Overlook at the south end of Great Island. There are many viewing opportunities along the first 0.5 mile of trail, but ambitious wildlife watchers can hike the entire 8-mile round-trip along beach, salt marsh, and pine uplands. Great Island separates Cape Cod Bay from Wellfleet Harbor. This marine environment is dictated by winds, waves, and tides.

Viewing Information: A path leads from the parking lot down to the salt marsh and to Great Island itself. Flocks of sea ducks such as goldeneyes, oldsquaws, and scoters are found seasonally on the Wellfleet Harbor side of the island. The forested uplands are home to white-tailed deer and eastern coyotes. Check for tracks in the sandy soil. Shorebirds, water birds, and crabs are the featured attractions on the spit and flats at the south end of the island near the Jeremy Point overlook. Black-bellied plovers, least sandpipers, and sanderlings share the shallows during migration with resident herring and great black-backed gulls. Spider, horseshoe, and fiddler crabs comb the flats in search of food. In winter, harbor seals congregate in numbers. *BE AWARE THAT AREAS SOUTH OF THE JEREMY POINT OVERLOOK ARE EXPOSED ONLY BRIEFLY AT LOW TIDE. USE CAUTION IN ALL TIDAL AREAS.*

Directions: *Follow signs from Route 6 to Wellfleet Center. Take Chequesset Neck Road along Wellfleet Harbor to the marked parking area.*

Ownership: NPS (508) 349-3785

Size: 1,000 acres   **Closest Town:** Wellfleet

SOUTHEAST

Description: Race Point lies at the northern extreme of Cape Cod, extending into the Atlantic Ocean adjacent to deep water. The upwelling currents here attract many fish, birds, and marine mammals. The ocean, beach, dune, salt marsh, and upland habitats all support diverse wildlife. Race Point also shelters Hatches Harbor, a tidal area with abundant opportunities to observe invertebrates in shallow water.

Viewing Information: A stop at Province Lands Visitor Center or Race Point Ranger Station will provide maps and information on access and points of interest. The ranger station is next to a short boardwalk with signs describing humpback, fin, and minke whales, all of which can be sighted just off the beach from late spring through early autumn. Schools of bluefish chase baitfish, and least terns make frequent dives in pursuit of sand lances. Fiddler and horseshoe crabs can be found in the shallows of Hatches Harbor along with periwinkles and shellfish. Birds of the open ocean, such as razorbills, kittiwakes, black guillemots, and gannets, can be seen in winter and early spring. Harbor seals winter along beaches and are often seen basking at low tide.

Directions: *From Route 6, follow Race Point Road for 1 mile to Province Lands Visitor Center. Race Point Road ends at the Race Point Beach parking area and ranger station.*

Ownership: NPS (508) 349-3785

Size: 1,372 acres   **Closest Town:** Provincetown

A humpback whale raises its flukes out of the water in a display known as "lobtailing." The purpose of lobtailing, breaching, fin slapping, and other behaviors is not well understood. BILL BYRNE

Description: On the surface, Stellwagen Bank appears identical to the surrounding waters of Cape Cod Bay and the Gulf of Maine. Underwater, however, a 117-square-mile plateau rises from the ocean floor to an average depth of 100 feet. This produces an upwelling of ocean currents and nutrients that results in a rich bloom of plankton, the foundation of the marine food web. Bottom-dwelling invertebrates, shellfish, and small finfish feed on the plankton and are in turn fed upon by larger predators including ground fish like cod, haddock, flounder; numerous resident and migratory sea birds; and summering great whales. Located 3 miles from Cape Cod to the south and 3 miles from Cape Ann to the north, Stellwagen Bank is accessible by boat from much of the Massachusetts coastline.

Viewing Information: Whale-watching cruises are the best public means of enjoying Stellwagen Bank. Contact the Massachusetts Office of Travel and Tourism to get up-to-date information and literature on boats leaving from Cape Ann, Boston, the south shore, and Cape Cod. Be prepared with extra clothing for sudden changes in weather. Binoculars and camera are recommended for up-close looks and photos of humpback, right, minke, and fin whales; Atlantic white-sided dolphins; or the occasional leatherback, loggerhead, or Atlantic ridley sea turtle. Anticipate a whale's spout or the flash of an extended fin or fluke, and look for irregularities in the surface of the sea which might indicate activity below. Bird life includes fulmars, shearwaters, petrels, gannets, gulls, razorbills, murres, and puffins. Watch for quick fly-bys or flocks of birds rafting together on the ocean surface. Many boats have naturalists on board who identify and describe the wildlife encountered. Research is conducted to identify individual whales and to learn about longevity, habitat needs, and reproduction. Information available from the Massachusetts Office of Travel and Tourism (617 727-3201) will include lists of whale-watching ships and their respective ports.

Ownership: NOAA (508) 747-1691 (Stellwagen Bank information)

Size: 842 square miles   **Closest Towns:** Provincetown & Gloucester

Be alert for wildlife while driving. Dawn and dusk can be particularly hazardous because of low light conditions and heightened animal activity. Serious injuries and fatalities occur following collisions with moose, bear, and deer. If a large animal crosses a road in front of you, watch for a second animal following close behind.

SOUTHEAST

95

WILDLIFE INDEX

The following is a partial list of popular wildlife species, groups of species, and some of the Viewing Sites where they occur: